fterwork
ookbook

afterwork
cookbook

no-fuss recipes for busy people

penguin books

PENGUIN BOOKS

Published by the Penguin Group
Penguin Group (Australia)
250 Camberwell Road, Camberwell, Victoria 3124, Australia
(a division of Pearson Australia Group Pty Ltd)
Penguin Group (USA) Inc.
375 Hudson Street, New York, New York 10014, USA
Penguin Group (Canada)
90 Eglinton Avenue East, Suite 700, Toronto ON M4P 2Y3, Canada
(a division of Pearson Penguin Canada Inc.)
Penguin Books Ltd
80 Strand, London WC2R 0RL, England
Penguin Ireland
25 St Stephen's Green, Dublin 2, Ireland
(a division of Penguin Books Ltd)
Penguin Books India Pvt Ltd
11 Community Centre, Panchsheel Park, New Delhi – 110 017, India
Penguin Group (NZ)
67 Apollo Drive, Mairangi Bay, Auckland 1310, New Zealand
(a division of Pearson New Zealand Ltd)
Penguin Books (South Africa) (Pty) Ltd
24 Sturdee Avenue, Rosebank, Johannesburg 2196, South Africa

Penguin Books Ltd, Registered Offices: 80 Strand, London, WC2R 0RL, England

First published by Penguin Group (Australia), 2007

10 9 8 7 6 5 4 3 2 1

Copyright © Penguin Group Australia 2007

The moral right of the author has been asserted

Many thanks to Matchbox Armadale, Dinosaur Designs and Market Imports for props.
Thanks also to Danielle Benson for her cooking.

Design by Elizabeth Theodosiadis © Penguin Group (Australia)
Photographs by Julie Renouf
Text by Victoria Heywood
Typeset in Nimbus Sans Novus by Post Pre-press Group, Brisbane, Queensland
Colour reproduction by Splitting Image, Clayton, Victoria
Printed in China by 1010 Printing International Limited

National Library of Australia
Cataloguing-in-Publication data:

  Afterwork Cookbook
  Includes index
  ISBN-13: 978 0 14 300518 6 (pbk)
  ISBN-10: 0 14 300518 9 (pbk)
  1. Quick and easy cookery

  641.555

www.penguin.com.au

contents

introduction

The key to fuss-free afterwork cooking is a well-stocked pantry – fill yours with a tempting selection of bottled, tinned and packaged foods and you'll be ready to whip up scrumptious meals and snacks in less time than it takes to order a takeaway pizza. A jar of char-grilled eggplant in oil, some black olive tapenade, dried pasta and a splash of olive oil and hey presto! – dinner is ready in ten minutes.

As well as being convenient and economical, pantry cookery tends to be more nutritious too, as it is generally lower in saturated fat and higher in fibre. (Think tuna and lentils, rather than a heavy meat casserole, or popcorn rather than fat-soaked chips). To help keep your meals healthy and balanced – even when you're cooking in a hurry – choose tinned vegetables and fruit with no added salt or sugar, tuna and salmon in spring water, and unsalted nuts and legumes such as baked beans.

Pantry cooking can help save you money, time and stress – whether you're using up items that have been sitting in the cupboard for a while, opting for vegetable or fish over expensive cuts of meat, or simply avoiding another unnecessary drive to the supermarket.

However, you don't have to sacrifice flavour, impact or style for convenience. Keep your pantry well stocked and you'll always have something tasty and impressive on hand to offer unexpected guests or to treat you and your family. For example, a block of good quality dark chocolate, carefully hidden in your pantry, can be used in so many ways – devoured as a luxury snack, grated onto vanilla ice-cream, or melted and mixed with liqueur, then drizzled over fruit for a spectacular dessert.

Naturally, you'll want to stock your pantry with the ingredients necessary for dishes you make time and time again – for example, pasta and the makings for a sauce, or flour, eggs and cocoa for quick muffins or a cake. However, your pantry should also be a source of inspiration for experimentation too. Half the fun is in trying new combinations of flavours and in making do with what's at hand.

When you're deciding what to cook, start with a foundation ingredient such as rice or pasta, then peek in the pantry and see what else you have. If your pantry has been stocked well, you'll be able to reach in and put together something delicious, nutritious – and fast.

This book contains over 100 recipes, using common ingredients like tinned tuna and frozen peas, as well as more exotic additions such as crab meat and water chestnuts. However, most dishes can be quickly assembled from the contents of the average pantry, along with a few refrigerator and freezer staples such as butter, bacon, parmesan cheese or frozen vegetables.

A full listing of the ingredients used in the recipes in this book is given in the next section (see page 5). At the back of the book you'll also find a handy shopping list with suggestions for stocking your pantry, fridge and freezer (see page 179). Use the list for inspiration, or photocopy it and stick it on the back of your pantry door as a handy checklist to refer to before you go grocery shopping. A weekly menu, relying purely on pantry, fridge and freezer staples, is also provided (see page 176).

the ultimate
pantry

Here is a list of ingredients that I believe all good pantries should contain. Once you've stocked up, you'll be able to make any of the recipes in this book at a moment's notice – and many more.

dairy

UHT (ultra heat treated) dairy products will keep pretty much indefinitely in the pantry but should be stored in the fridge and used within a couple of days once opened.

essential dairy:

- UHT long-life milk
- UHT long-life cream
- UHT long-life custard

oils

All oils should be stored in the pantry, away from light, air and temperature fluctuations, or they can turn rancid. It's a good idea to keep a variety of oils on hand for different uses – extra virgin olive oil for salad dressings and Italian dishes, sesame oil for Asian recipes like stir-fries, and vegetable or peanut oil for frying. Canola oil spray is handy for greasing baking pans, while olive oil spray can be used to give vegetables a light coating before roasting.

essential oils:

- olive oil – virgin, extra virgin, flavoured (with garlic/chilli etc.)
- peanut oil
- sesame oil
- vegetable, canola or sunflower oil

sauces, pastes and condiments

Sauces, pastes, vinegars and condiments generally store very well – sometimes for a number of years – but check labelling on the bottle to see if it needs to be refrigerated once opened. Small sachets of tomato paste are handy, as you use all the paste at one go, and avoid wastage. (If using a tin or jar of tomato paste, freeze any that is left over in ice-cube trays, then store the frozen cubes in a plastic bag.)

essential sauces, pastes, vinegars and condiments:

- fish sauce
- golden syrup
- harissa or chilli paste
- honey
- lime pickle
- mango chutney
- maple syrup
- mayonnaise
- mustard – Dijon, English, wholegrain
- onion marmalade
- satay sauce
- soy sauce
- sweet chilli sauce
- tahini
- tomato paste
- tomato relish
- tomato sauce
- vanilla extract or essence
- Vegemite
- vinegar – balsamic, cider, red and/or white wine
- Worcestershire sauce

tins and jars

Preserving food in oil, brine, salt, sugar or alcohol is an age-old way of keeping food edible way past its normal lifespan. For the afterwork cook, tins and jars of sweet and savoury goodies are a must. A simple jar of apricots in liqueur or a tin of peaches make an easy dessert, should unexpected guests arrive. Tins of fish and jars of vegetables preserved in oil can form the backbone of many a casserole, pasta sauce or risotto, or be served as part of an antipasto platter. Strongly flavoured savoury titbits such as sun-dried tomatoes and anchovies also increase your cooking options and can transform a pizza or salad into something really special.

Tinned beans, peas and lentils are another pantry essential, as they are economical, packed full of protein, and endlessly versatile. Whiz into a dip, bake in a hearty casserole, purée into soup, or serve in a salad or vegetarian dish.

Most tinned food will keep very well, although it's generally recommended to use tins within a year of purchase. Once opened, transfer any leftovers into an airtight container, store in the fridge and use within a couple of days.

essential tins and jars:

- anchovy fillets in oil
- anchovy paste
- artichoke hearts in oil
- baby corn
- basil pesto
- bean sprouts
- beans – borlotti, butter, cannellini, red kidney, pinto, etc.
- beetroot
- black olive paste
- capers
- chickpeas
- champignons
- coconut milk
- coconut cream
- corn kernels
- crab meat
- fruit – apricots, peaches, pears, cherries, etc.
- garlic – crushed
- gherkins
- ginger – crushed
- ham
- jalapeno peppers
- jams
- lentils – red, green, yellow and/or brown
- marmalade
- mushrooms
- olives – green and black, pitted, whole and stuffed
- passata
- peanut butter
- prawns in brine
- preserved lemon
- red capsicum slices in oil
- salmon
- sardines
- sun-dried tomatoes
- tapenade
- tomato paste
- tomatoes – chopped, crushed, diced, whole peeled, etc.
- tuna in oil or brine
- water chestnuts

dry ingredients

Dried pulses such as lentils, peas and beans keep for ages but as most need to be soaked for at least a few hours before cooking, it's wise to stock some pre-cooked tinned pulses for speedy meals.

Pasta is another key ingredient for many dishes, and while fresh pasta is more flavoursome and faster to cook, dried pasta is perfectly acceptable. Keep a variety on hand – lasagne sheets, spaghetti, fettuccini, penne, spirals, shells, etc. Grains such as polenta and instant couscous are handy too, while rice and noodles of different types are widely used in Asian cookery.

Some dry ingredients, such as fruit and nuts, do not last particularly well once opened, so buy in small quantities and be sure to keep in an airtight container.

essential dry ingredients:

- almonds – whole, ground, slivered
- breadcrumbs
- burghul (cracked wheat)
- cashews
- bicarbonate of soda
- brown sugar
- castor sugar
- cereal
- Chinese crispy noodles
- chocolate – block and chips
- coffee – instant, whole roasted beans or ground
- corn chips and/or taco shells
- cornflour
- couscous
- crackers
- currants
- dates
- dried fruit – apricots, apples, etc.
- dried Porcini and chanterelle mushrooms
- egg or wheat noodles
- glass noodles or vermicelli
- icing sugar
- lentils – red, green, yellow and/or brown
- panettone (Italian sweet bread with dried fruit)
- pasta – macaroni, pappardelle, penne, spirals, spaghetti, fettuccini, etc.
- peanuts (unsalted)
- pine nuts
- plain flour (white and wholemeal)
- polenta
- popcorn kernels
- raisins
- rice – basmati, jasmine, long and short grain, brown and white
- risotto rice (Arborio)
- rolled oats
- self-raising flour (white and wholemeal)
- semolina
- sponge fingers
- sugar
- sultanas
- tea (black tea, green tea and herbal)
- walnuts
- yeast

stock

Stock is great for whipping up a quick soup or risotto, or adding oomph to a sauce or gravy. It's up to you whether you use frozen home-made stock, powdered stock, stock cubes or a long-life liquid stock. Keep a variety of flavours on hand.

essential stocks:

- beef stock
- chicken stock
- fish stock
- vegetable stock

alcohol

Wine, liqueurs, and sometimes beer are all used for flavour in cooking – not to mention keeping the chef happy. White wine is great in risotto, while rice wine or mirin can be used in many Asian dishes. Brandy or Cointreau is a great standby for a pantry dessert. Just add a splash to tinned or frozen fruit, or drizzle over pancakes for an impressive end to an impromptu meal.

essential alcohol:

- beer
- brandy or other liqueur of choice
- rice wine or mirin
- sherry
- wine – white and red

herbs, spices and seasonings

Herbs, spices and seasonings pack a powerful punch in terms of adding flavour and aroma to a dish, although most have very little nutritional value. Fresh spices are best, so buy only small quantities of ground or dried spices at a time and store in airtight containers in the pantry. A spice rack will let you see what you have at a glance, and what you may need to stock up on.

Herbs such as parsley, basil, chives and coriander taste far better fresh than dried, so consider growing your own in the garden or in a pot on the kitchen windowsill. You can also buy tubes of freshly chopped herbs at the supermarket nowadays, which are far better than dried herbs, but still no substitute for the real thing. These tubes need to be kept in the fridge once opened. To extend their life, keep them in the freezer – you don't need to defrost them, just add them to your cooking still frozen, and return the tube to the freezer straight away.

essential herbs, spices and seasonings:

- allspice
- basil
- bay leaves
- black peppercorns
- cayenne pepper
- chilli – flakes or ground
- chicken salt
- chives
- cinnamon – sticks and ground
- cloves
- coriander
- cumin
- curry powder
- five-spice powder
- kaffir lime leaves
- lemon pepper

- marjoram
- mixed herbs
- nutmeg
- oregano
- paprika
- poppy seeds
- rosemary
- saffron – powder or threads
- sea salt
- sesame seeds
- star anise
- thyme
- Thai curry paste – green and red
- turmeric
- vanilla beans

vegetables

Not all vegetables have to be kept in the refrigerator. In fact, potatoes, sweet potatoes, onions and garlic do best when kept in a cool, dark, well-ventilated spot – such as an open rack in your pantry. Other vegetables, like carrots, will keep for a number of weeks in the crisper section of your fridge. Keep a plentiful supply of these vegetables on hand, as well as whatever fruit is in season, and you'll be able to whip up any number of delicious meals with no fuss.

Crushed garlic can be bought in a jar (keep in the fridge once opened), but although it's convenient, it tastes nowhere near as good as fresh cloves. Lemons and limes also store well, and are an essential part of many dishes. Again, lemon juice in a bottle is handy, but doesn't have quite the zing of the real thing.

essential vegetables:

- carrots
- garlic
- lemons
- limes
- onions – brown and red (Spanish)
- potatoes
- pumpkin
- sweet potatoes

from the garden

A simple pot of herbs on the balcony or in a corner of the garden can become an essential part of your kitchen. Fresh herbs can transform an otherwise ordinary dish, and if you have room for some fast-growing salad greens such as rocket and spinach, all the better.

essential herbs:

- basil
- chives
- coriander
- marjoram
- mint
- oregano
- parsley
- salad greens
- thyme
- rosemary

refrigerator essentials

Eggs should be stored in a carton in the fridge, but not in the egg racks in the door, as the temperature varies too much. Store eggs with the pointy end down as this helps keep the yolk intact when you separate them for cooking. Always take eggs out of the fridge an hour before using to allow them to reach room temperature, particularly if you are using them for baking or plan on whipping the egg whites.

Cheeses are a handy fridge staple, and mozzarella, cheddar and other yellow cheeses keep for several weeks. Hard cheeses such as parmesan can keep for much longer, particularly if ungrated. Wrap cheese in waxed paper rather than plastic, which makes it sweat. Grated cheese can be kept in the freezer until needed.

refrigerator essentials:

- butter
- cheese – mozzarella, cheddar, tasty, parmesan
- chorizo or similar cured spicy sausage
- eggs
- feta
- milk
- natural yoghurt
- salami
- sour cream

freezer essentials

Although many dishes can be prepared without dipping into the freezer at all, it is useful to keep a supply of frozen vegetables such as peas, which taste much better than the tinned or dried variety and maintain much of their nutritional value. Other handy things to stock in the freezer include berries or fruit, a selection of breads, and ice-cream for an instant dessert or guilty pleasure. Fish and chicken fillets also freeze well, and have been included in several recipes within this book. An easy way to store bacon and pancetta is to roll up each slice, place on a tray and freeze. Once frozen, store the rolls in a plastic bag in the freezer.

freezer essentials:

- bacon or pancetta
- berries – blueberries, strawberries, raspberries, etc.
- broad beans
- broccoli florets
- chicken fillets
- ciabatta or similar crusty loaf
- corn kernels
- fish fillets
- green beans
- ice-cream
- peas
- pita bread
- souvlaki bread
- spinach
- prawns
- puff pastry
- shortcrust pastry

substitutions

Don't panic if you don't have exactly the ingredients listed in these recipes; you can improvise with whatever you do have to hand. For example, broad beans instead of peas for a risotto, butter beans instead of borlotti beans for a casserole. After all, half the fun of quick afterwork cooking is making the most of what you have!

There are also a number of accepted substitutions you can make when cooking:

- To make your own self-raising flour, mix 1 cup of plain flour with 2 teaspoons of baking powder.

- 1 teaspoon of baking powder can be made from ¼ teaspoon bicarbonate of soda mixed with ½ teaspoon cream of tartar.

- Margarine can be substituted for butter, as long as you don't use 'light' margarine, which has a much lower fat content and will not give the same result.

- Evaporated milk can be swapped for cream. If you chill it in the freezer for an hour or so, it can even be whipped.

- ½ cup butter mixed with ¾ cup milk substitutes for 1 cup cream when baking or cooking.

- If you don't have any coconut milk, try adding a few drops of coconut essence to evaporated milk. Coconut cream can also be reconstituted into coconut milk with the addition of water.

- In savoury dishes, use natural yoghurt instead of cream. However, add only at the last minute and do not boil, or the yoghurt may curdle and separate.

- 1 cup of honey can be substituted with 1¼ cups sugar and ¼ cup liquid, but the flavour will be slightly different.

- Instead of using dried breadcrumbs, use finely ground crackers or crushed cereal like Weet-Bix or Weeties.

- 30 g chocolate is equivalent to 3 tablespoons cocoa and 1 tablespoon melted butter.

smart pantry management

When re-stocking your pantry, remember to keep new items at the back of the pantry so you use products with an older use-by date first. Grouping similar products together – for example, a shelf for flours, cocoa, baking powder, etc., and another for pasta, tinned tomatoes and jars of goodies – means you can easily lay your hands on things you need. If space is at a premium, consider installing racks on the back of the pantry door (fixed or over-door hanging shelves) to increase your storage options. These narrow shelves can be useful for storing small packets, bottles and jars.

Once packets of dry goods have been opened, it's a good idea to decant them into airtight containers to keep the food fresh and any hungry critters out. Colourless plastic or glass makes it easy to see what you have and what you need to stock up on. Failing that, invest in a decent label-maker, or some stylish container labels. Be sure to mark the different types of flour clearly, as many a cooking disaster has resulted from the accidental use of plain rather than self-raising flour.

cheese twists

snacks and starters

bruschetta

Serves: 4–6 **Preparation:** 3 minutes **Cooking:** 2 minutes

1 loaf crusty bread (preferably ciabatta)
2 cloves garlic, peeled
½ cup extra virgin olive oil
salt

1 Slice the loaf on an angle into thick slices. Toast each side on a dry cast-iron griddle, or under the griller.

2 Rub one side with garlic, then drizzle with olive oil. Season and eat immediately.

extra topping suggestions
- diced tomato, spanish onion and basil
- red capsicum slices in oil, drained
- artichoke hearts in oil, drained
- mashed anchovies and capers

cheese twists

Makes: 32 **Preparation:** 8 minutes **Cooking:** 10 minutes

2 sheets puff pastry
2 eggs, beaten
6 tablespoons finely grated parmesan cheese
2 tablespoons poppy or sesame seeds

1 Preheat oven to 210°C and lightly grease two baking trays.

2 Lightly brush the pastry sheets with the egg. Cut pastry into long strips, about 1.5 cm wide.

3 Take hold of a pastry strip at each end, and twist gently a couple of times. Place on the baking tray. Repeat with the rest of the pastry strips.

4 Sprinkle the twists with cheese and poppy seeds and bake for 10 minutes unti puffed and golden.

ciabatta crispbread

Serves: 6 as a dip accompaniment **Preparation:** 10 minutes **Cooking:** 5 minutes

extra virgin olive oil
mix of herbs and spices – garlic, rosemary, chives, oregano, dried chilli flakes etc.
1 stale ciabatta loaf (or use souvlaki bread)

1 Mix the oil with the seasoning ingredients and let sit for about 10 minutes. Cut loaf into very thin slices (or souvlaki bread into triangular pieces) and place on a baking tray. Brush each slice with the flavoured oil, then toast in a low oven until crisp and golden on both sides.

2 Serve with dips, pâté, cheese or deli meats.

corn fritters

Serves: 4 **Preparation:** 5 minutes **Cooking:** 10 minutes

2 cups plain flour
salt
1 teaspoon bicarbonate of soda
1½ cups milk
1 egg
1 × 420 g tin corn kernels, drained (or use frozen)
1 tablespoon finely chopped fresh parsley
vegetable oil

1 Sift flour, salt and bicarbonate of soda into a basin. Make a well in the centre and add the milk and egg. Whisk to combine. Stir in the corn kernels and parsley.

2 Heat a little oil in a heavy-based frying pan and fry spoonfuls of batter until bubbles appear on the surface of the mixture. Flip the fritters over and cook the other side.

3 Serve with tomato relish, onion marmalade, sautéed onions, and/or crisp bacon.

hummus

Serves: 4–6 **Preparation:** 5 minutes

2 cloves garlic, roughly chopped
1 × 440-g tin chickpeas, drained
juice of 1 lemon
black pepper
¼ – ⅓ cup tahini
pinch of paprika, to serve

1 Whiz garlic and chickpeas together in the food processor, then add lemon juice, pepper and tahini, processing until smooth. Transfer to serving bowl and garnish with paprika.

2 Serve with crackers, grissini, toasted bread, pita or vegetable sticks made from whatever you have in the fridge – carrots, cucumber, capsicum or celery.

lentil terrine

Serves: 6–8 **Preparation:** 10 minutes **Cooking:** 20 minutes

1 onion, finely chopped
2 tablespoons olive oil
2 cups dried red or green lentils
2 tablespoons natural yoghurt, tahini or sour cream
1 clove garlic, crushed
½ teaspoon salt
3 tablespoons lemon juice
¼ teaspoon ground cumin
¼ teaspoon ground coriander

1 Sauté the onion in the olive oil until golden. Meanwhile, heat a large saucepan of salted water and cook the lentils until soft (about 20 minutes).

2 Put the lentils and onions in a food processor with all the other ingredients and whiz to a smooth paste. Add some olive oil if the mixture is too thick.

3 Pour into a serving dish and serve with crackers, bread or vegetable sticks.

pissaladière

Serves: 6 **Preparation:** 30 minutes **Cooking:** 20 minutes

2 tablespoons olive oil
5 onions, sliced thinly
2 cloves garlic, finely sliced
pinch of dried thyme
½ cup tinned chopped tomatoes
250 g puff pastry
8 anchovy fillets in oil, drained
12 black olives, pitted and halved

1 Preheat oven to 230°C.

2 Heat the oil in a saucepan and cook the onions, garlic and thyme over a moderate heat until the onions are soft and golden. Stir in the tomatoes, raise the heat and cook until thickened (about 5 minutes).

3 On a floured surface, roll out the pastry into an oblong about 28 cm × 35 cm. Prick it all over with a fork and slide onto a greased baking tray. Leave it to rest for 20 minutes.

4 Spread the tomato mix over the pastry, all the way to the edges. Scatter the anchovies and olives on top. Bake for about 20 minutes or until the base is crispy.

pizza base

Serves: 2 **Preparation:** 10 minutes **Cooking:** 25 minutes

2 cups self-raising flour
¼ teaspoon salt
30 g butter, chopped into little pieces
1 cup milk
1 tablespoon oil
tomato paste

1 Preheat oven to 180°C.

2 Sift flour and salt into a bowl, add butter and rub in until it resembles breadcrumbs. Add the milk and knead to a soft dough.

3 Roll out the dough until it forms a circle roughly 35 cm across. Brush with oil, then spread with tomato paste and add your favourite toppings. Cook for 20–25 minutes.

suggested toppings

Artichoke hearts in oil, olives, chorizo, smoked ham, salami, bacon, anchovies, sardines, sun-dried tomatoes, capers, onion, dried herbs, egg, red capsicum in oil, grilled eggplant in oil, grated tasty cheese, feta, mozzarella.

poptastic popcorn

Serves: 4 **Preparation:** 2 minutes **Cooking:** 5 minutes

1 cup popcorn kernels
2 tablespoons vegetable oil
½ cup butter, melted
salt
seasoning of your choice – chicken seasoning,
    lemon pepper, mixed herbs etc.

1 Heat the oil in a large saucepan (with lid). Add the popcorn and immediately place the lid on top. Once the corn starts popping, give the saucepan an occasional shake to prevent the kernels sticking and burning. Remove from the heat as soon as the sound of popping subsides.

2 Pour over the melted butter, add salt and seasoning to taste, and serve while still warm.

salmon sandwiches

Makes: 16 small sandwiches **Preparation:** 10 minutes

1 × 200-g tin salmon, drained and flaked
½ red onion, finely chopped
3 tablespoons mayonnaise
zest of 1 lemon, finely grated
1 tablespoon finely chopped fresh parsley
salt and freshly ground black pepper
butter
16 slices bread

1 Mix the salmon, onion, mayonnaise, lemon zest and parsley together. Season with salt and pepper to taste.

2 Butter the bread and spread the salmon mixture on eight slices. Make into sandwiches, trim crusts, and cut into halves to serve.

savoury omelette with bacon

Serves: 1–2 **Preparation:** 2 minutes **Cooking:** 8 minutes

2 eggs
salt and freshly ground black pepper
1 tablespoon chopped fresh herbs or 1 teaspoon
    dried mixed herbs (optional)
1 tablespoon butter
2 rashers bacon, grilled until crispy

1 Break the eggs into a bowl and whisk lightly. Season with salt and pepper and herbs.

2 Melt the butter in a frying pan. When it starts to froth, tip in the egg mix and tilt the pan to make sure the egg covers the base. Once the egg has started setting around the edges, use a wooden spoon to move the cooked portion to the centre. Tilt again to allow the uncooked egg to move to the edges.

3 After a couple of minutes, spoon your choice of fillings into the centre, then flip one third of the omelette over the filling. Remove from the heat and slide the omelette onto a plate, flipping the remaining third over the rest of the filling to enclose it completely.

4 Serve immediately, with the crispy grilled bacon on the side.

suggested fillings
- 2 tablespoons grated tasty cheese
- 2 tablespoons cubed feta cheese
- 1 tablespoon grated white onion or sliced spring onion

savoury palmiers

Makes: 36 **Preparation:** 10 minutes **Cooking:** 10 minutes

2 sheets ready-rolled frozen puff pastry, defrosted
basil pesto, anchovy paste or any other savoury paste

1 Preheat oven to 200°C and grease two oven trays.

2 Cut each pastry sheet in half and spread with your choice of savoury paste.

3 Fold the long edges of the pastry in towards the middle, then fold the pastry in half again. Slice the log into thin slices and place on the oven trays.

4 Bake for 10 minutes or until pastry is puffed and golden.

sesame prawn toasts

Makes: 32 **Preparation:** 10 minutes **Cooking:** 10 minutes **Standing:** 30 minutes

8 slices white bread
350 g cooked peeled prawns (either tinned
   and drained, or frozen and defrosted)
½ onion, finely grated
1 teaspoon crushed ginger (fresh or from a jar)
½ teaspoon sugar
1 egg, beaten
3 teaspoons rice wine or sherry
1 tablespoon soy sauce
1 tablespoon sesame oil
1 teaspoon salt
freshly ground black pepper
2 tablespoons sesame seeds
oil for frying

1 Preheat oven to 200°C. Bake bread for a few minutes until slightly hardened.

2 Whiz the prawns in a food processor until smooth. Add all the other ingredients except the sesame seeds and blend until the paste is smooth. Leave to rest for at least 30 minutes, then use your hands to squeeze out excess moisture.

3 Mix the paste and spread evenly over the bread slices. Sprinkle with sesame seeds, trim crusts and cut each slice into four triangles or use a biscuit cutter to make rounds.

4 Heat a good layer of oil (about 5 mm) in a wok or frying pan and fry the toast in batches, spread side down, until golden. Turn and fry the other side briefly, then remove with a slotted spoon and drain on kitchen paper before serving.

spiced nuts

Serves: 4 **Preparation:** 3 minutes **Cooking:** 7 minutes

This dish can also be made with other combinations of spices, such as cumin and paprika.

250 g raw unsalted mixed nuts (cashews,
    peanuts, almonds, pecans, etc.)
½ teaspoon five-spice powder
1 teaspoon vegetable oil
salt

1 Preheat oven to 180°C and line a baking tray with baking paper.

2 In a bowl, mix the nuts with the other ingredients until well coated. Scatter onto the baking tray and bake for 7 minutes or until golden and toasted.

3 Cool before serving.

tahini dip

Serves: 6 **Preparation:** 5 minutes

Tahini is a paste made of crushed sesame seeds. It can be used as a spread, like peanut butter or as a dip, as shown below. You can also use it as an accompaniment to meat or as topping for a baked potato.

1 cup tahini
¾ cup water
1–3 cloves garlic, crushed
juice of ½ a lemon
½ teaspoon ground cumin (optional)
½ teaspoon salt
1 tablespoon chopped fresh parsley, to serve

1 Blend tahini in a bowl with just enough water to make a smooth, whitish paste about the consistency of mayonnaise.

2 Mix garlic with the lemon juice, cumin and salt and stir into the tahini cream. Taste and adjust for seasoning.

3 Serve with parsley scattered on top.

tapenade

Makes: 1 cup **Preparation:** 5 minutes

1 cup pitted black olives
2 anchovy fillets in oil, drained
2 cloves garlic, crushed
3 tablespoons olive oil
1 tablespoon finely chopped basil
½ tablespoon capers, rinsed

1 Place all ingredients in a food processor and blend until smooth.

2 Taste and adjust the balance of ingredients to suit your personal preferences (e.g. add a few more capers, or a little more garlic if you prefer it that way).

welsh rarebit

Serves: 4 **Preparation:** 5 minutes **Cooking:** 5 minutes

125 g cheddar cheese, finely grated
1 tablespoon butter, softened
2 teaspoons English or French mustard
1 egg, beaten
1 tablespoon beer (optional)
1 teaspoon Worcestershire sauce
salt and freshly ground black pepper
8 slices bread
dried chilli flakes, to serve (optional)

1 Mix together the cheese, butter, mustard, egg, beer and Worcestershire sauce. Season to taste.

2 Toast the bread and spread generously with the mixture. Grill under a hot grill until golden brown and bubbling. Sprinkle with chilli flakes if desired.

white bean dip

Serves: 8 **Preparation:** 5 minutes

1 × 400-g tin cannellini or butter beans, drained
1 clove garlic
2 tablespoons olive oil
zest of 2 lemons
juice of 1 lemon
1 teaspoon salt
1 tablespoon finely chopped fresh herbs – thyme, rosemary or parsley

1 Put all ingredients into a blender or food processor and blend until smooth. (The herbs can be added after blending if you'd like more texture.) Taste and adjust salt.

onion soup

soups

asian chicken dumpling soup

Serves: 4 **Preparation:** 10 minutes **Cooking:** 20 minutes

6 cups chicken stock
2 star anise
1 cinnamon stick
2 tablespoons soy sauce
1 teaspoon crushed ginger (fresh or from a jar)
2 chicken breast fillets, poached and shredded

dumplings
⅔ cup water
1 tablespoon butter
pinch of salt
1 clove garlic, crushed
½ cup semolina
1 egg, beaten
½ teaspoon dried basil leaves (or two tablespoons
    finely chopped fresh basil)

1 To make the soup, place the stock, star anise, cinnamon, soy and ginger into a saucepan and simmer for 5 minutes.

2 To make the dumplings, combine water with the butter, salt and garlic in a saucepan over a medium heat. Bring to the boil, then add the semolina in a steady stream, while whisking briskly. Add egg and basil. Cook for 3 minutes, stirring all the time, until the semolina starts to come away from the sides of the pan.

3 Heat the soup until it is very hot but not boiling. Roll tablespoonfuls of the dumpling mixture into balls and drop into the soup. Cook for 5 minutes, turning once, then remove dumplings with a slotted spoon and place into serving bowls.

4 Warm the shredded chicken in the soup mixture for a couple of minutes, then ladle the soup over the dumplings.

chickpea soup

Serves: 6 **Preparation:** 10 minutes **Cooking:** 30 minutes

1 tablespoon butter
1 onion, chopped
175 g bacon or pancetta, chopped
1 carrot, chopped
1 celery stick, chopped (optional)
2 × 400-g tins chickpeas, drained
1 litre chicken, vegetable or beef stock
salt and freshly ground black pepper
6 slices of bread
freshly grated parmesan cheese, to serve

1 In a large saucepan, melt the butter and fry the onion, bacon, carrot and celery until the vegetables are soft.

2 Add the chickpeas and mix well. Pour in the stock and season with salt and pepper. Cover and simmer for about 30 minutes until the chickpeas are very tender.

3 Toast and butter the bread, then place in the bottom of each soup bowl. Pour over the soup, then sprinkle with a little parmesan.

corn chowder

Serves: 4 **Preparation:** 5 minutes **Cooking:** 30 minutes

2 tablespoons olive oil
1 onion, finely chopped
1 potato, finely diced
1 cup chicken or vegetable stock
1 tablespoon butter
1 tablespoon plain flour
2½ cups milk
1 × 420-g tin corn kernels (or use frozen)
cayenne pepper
salt and freshly ground black pepper
finely chopped fresh parsley, to serve
3 rashers bacon, grilled till crisp then crumbled, to serve

1 Heat the olive oil in a large pan and sauté the onion. Add the potato and stock and cook over a medium heat for around 10 minutes.

2 In another saucepan, make a white sauce – mix the butter, flour and milk together and whisk constantly over a medium heat until the sauce is smooth and has thickened.

3 Add the white sauce and corn to the potato mixture and cook for a further 15 minutes, stirring constantly to prevent burning. Season to taste with cayenne pepper, and salt and black pepper.

4 Serve with parsley and bacon strewn over the top.

curried thai lentil soup

Serves: 6 **Preparation:** 10 minutes **Cooking:** 60 minutes

splash of olive oil
1 onion, chopped
1 tablespoon Thai green curry paste
1 cup dried green lentils
4 cups water
2 cups coconut milk or coconut cream
1 tablespoon soft brown sugar
4 kaffir lime leaves, shredded
salt and freshly ground black pepper

1 Fry the onion and curry paste in oil until well browned, then add the lentils, water, coconut milk, sugar and kaffir lime leaves.

2 Bring to the boil, season to taste and simmer for 45 minutes or until lentils are soft. Cool, then purée until smooth.

variation
Try adding a small tin of baby corn or water chestnuts for a more substantial soup.

onion soup

Serves: 6 **Preparation:** 10 minutes **Cooking:** 45 minutes

1 tablespoon butter
750 g onions, finely sliced
2 cloves garlic, finely chopped
2 litres vegetable stock (chicken or beef are also fine)
1 cup white wine
1 teaspoon thyme
1 bay leaf
½ teaspoon cinnamon
salt and freshly ground black pepper
12 slices stale baguette or other bread, to serve (optional)
grated tasty cheese, to serve

1 In a heavy-based saucepan, melt the butter and cook the onion over a slow heat until golden brown (about 20 minutes).

2 Add the garlic and cook for a couple of minutes. Gradually add the stock and wine, stirring continuously. Add the herbs, cinnamon and season with salt and pepper, then cover the pan and simmer for a further 20 minutes.

3 To serve, toast the bread and place in the bottom of each soup bowl. Ladle over the soup and sprinkle with cheese.

4 Place under a grill until the cheese turns golden. Serve immediately.

pea and parmesan soup

Serves: 4 **Preparation:** 5 minutes **Cooking:** 10 minutes

1 litre chicken or vegetable stock
700 g frozen peas
1 red onion, finely chopped (or use a brown onion)
⅓ cup olive oil
salt and freshly ground black pepper
parmesan cheese, to serve
olive oil, to serve

1 Bring the stock to the boil and cook the peas in it for about 5 minutes.

2 In another pan, sauté the onion in the olive oil until soft. Stir the onion into the pea mixture, and simmer for a couple of minutes longer.

3 Season to taste. Blend in a food processor.

4 Serve either warm or cold, dressed with a shaving of parmesan and a splash of olive oil.

potato soup

Serves: 6 **Preparation:** 10 minutes **Cooking:** 20 minutes

⅓ cup olive oil
4 large potatoes, peeled and diced
1 onion, thinly sliced
½ teaspoon dried rosemary
1.2 litres chicken or vegetable stock
salt and freshly ground black pepper

1 Sauté the potatoes, onion and rosemary in the oil until the onion softens. Then pour in the stock and stir thoroughly. Cover, bring to the boil and simmer for 20 minutes until the potatoes are soft.

2 Purée with a hand-held blender or in a food processor, and add salt and pepper to taste.

rag soup (stracciatella)

Serves: 6 **Preparation:** 10 minutes **Cooking:** 5 minutes

1 litre chicken stock
3 eggs
½ cup finely grated parmesan cheese
1 tablespoon finely chopped fresh parsley
½ teaspoon nutmeg
salt and freshly ground black pepper

1 Bring the chicken stock to the boil in a large saucepan. Meanwhile, whisk the eggs, cheese, parsley and nutmeg together. Season with salt and pepper.

2 Add the egg mix to the boiling stock. Once lightly set, stir with a fork until the egg separates into long strands or 'rags' – after which this Italian soup is named.

sweet potato and coconut soup

Serves: 6 **Preparation:** 10 minutes **Cooking:** 20 minutes

3 tablespoons vegetable oil
1 onion, finely chopped
750 g sweet potato (kumara), peeled and chopped
1 carrot, peeled and chopped
2 cups vegetable or chicken stock
½ cup coconut milk
1 tablespoon sweet chilli sauce
yoghurt or sour cream, to serve

1 Heat oil in a saucepan and fry the onion, sweet potato and carrot for about 5 minutes. Add the stock and cook until the sweet potato is tender.

2 Add the coconut milk and chilli sauce and use a hand-held blender or food processor to blend until smooth.

3 Serve topped with a dollop of natural yoghurt or sour cream.

pappardelle with grilled capsicum, capers and olives

seafood

anchovy pasta

Serves: 4 **Preparation:** 10 minutes **Cooking:** 15 minutes

12 anchovy fillets in oil, drained
3 cloves garlic, finely chopped
2 tablespoons chopped fresh parsley
3 tablespoons olive oil
salt and freshly ground black pepper
100 g breadcrumbs
500 g pasta of your choice
extra breadcrumbs, to serve
25 g pine nuts, lightly toasted, to serve (optional)

1 Mash anchovies into a smooth paste with a few drops of water. Add the garlic, parsley and most of the olive oil. Season to taste.

2 Toast the breadcrumbs in a pan over a medium heat until golden brown. Add the remaining oil and toss to coat.

3 Cook the pasta in a large saucepan of boiling salted water until al dente. Drain and stir through the anchovy sauce. Add a little warm water if the sauce seems too dry.

4 Sprinkle with breadcrumbs and pine nuts before serving.

fish cakes

Serves: 2–3 **Preparation:** 15 minutes **Cooking:** 30 minutes

2 cups mashed potatoes
½ tablespoon Thai curry paste (optional)
milk
1 × 425-g tin tuna or salmon, drained and flaked
salt and freshly ground black pepper
1 egg, beaten
2 cups dried breadcrumbs
oil for frying
soy sauce or sweet chilli sauce, to serve

1 In a saucepan, blend the mashed potato with the curry paste and a little milk and stir over moderate heat until smooth. Add fish and season to taste.

2 Leave mixture to cool, then shape into small rissoles.

3 Dip the fish cakes into the egg and then coat with breadcrumbs. Fry in hot oil until golden brown, or bake in the oven for 15 minutes or until cooked.

4 Serve with soy sauce or sweet chilli sauce for dipping.

garlic prawns with noodles

Serves: 4 **Preparation:** 10 minutes **Cooking:** 5 minutes

¼ cup peanut oil

1 teaspoon dried chilli flakes

2 cloves garlic, chopped

500 g uncooked frozen prawns, defrosted

200 g egg noodles, cooked

2 tablespoons soy sauce

2 tablespoons sweet chilli sauce

1 Heat the oil and gently fry the chilli and garlic for a minute or so. Add the prawns and cook until pink (about 3 minutes).

2 Toss with the egg noodles, soy and sweet chilli sauce. Continue cooking until heated through.

lemon cod

Serves: 6 **Preparation:** 5 minutes **Cooking:** 10 minutes

2 tablespoons plain flour
6 large frozen cod fillets (or other firm white fish), defrosted
3 tablespoons butter
juice of 1 lemon
⅓ cup dry white wine
salt and freshly ground black pepper
lemon wedges, to serve

1 Put the flour into a plastic bag, add the fish fillets and shake until well coated.

2 Melt the butter in a wide frying pan and fry the fish for 2 minutes on each side (slightly more for thicker fillets). Remove fish from pan and keep warm until required.

3 Pour the lemon juice and wine into the frying pan and boil rapidly for a few minutes. Use a wooden spoon to stir in any crispy bits stuck to the base.

4 Replace the fish in the pan and warm through, spooning the sauce over the fish.

5 Serve with lemon wedges.

mediterranean prawn stew

Serves: 4 **Preparation:** 10 minutes **Cooking:** 15 minutes

This rich prawn stew can also be used as a topping for pasta, or can be served over boiled potatoes.

2 tablespoons olive oil
2 onions, sliced
4 cloves garlic, finely chopped
2 × 410-g tin crushed tomatoes
1 cup white wine
2 cups fish or vegetable stock
500 g frozen uncooked prawns, defrosted
2 tablespoons chopped fresh parsley
salt and freshly ground black pepper

1 Heat the oil in a casserole dish or large saucepan over a moderate heat. Add the onion and garlic and cook until golden and caramelised. Add the tomatoes, wine and stock and simmer until slightly thickened.

2 Toss in the prawns and cook for about 5 minutes or until they turn pink and are cooked through; don't overcook or they will become chewy. Add the parsley and season to taste.

3 Serve with crusty bread.

noodles with prawn relish

Serves: 4 **Preparation:** 10 minutes **Cooking:** 2 minutes

150 g rice vermicelli or glass noodles

relish
250 g cooked peeled prawns (frozen or from a tin), finely chopped
1 tablespoon satay sauce
16 tinned water chestnuts, finely chopped
1 tablespoon crushed ginger (fresh or from a jar)
3 teaspoons fish sauce
2 tablespoons lemon or lime juice
1 teaspoon dried chilli flakes
cucumber strips, mint leaves and tinned bean sprouts, to serve (optional)

1 Soak noodles in hot water until soft, then rinse and drain.

2 Mix together all the relish ingredients.

3 Pile the noodles into four bowls and top with the relish.

4 Garnish with cucumber, mint leaves and bean sprouts – or whatever fresh herbs you have to hand.

oliver's olive pasta

Serves: 4 **Preparation:** 10 minutes **Cooking:** 15 minutes

300 g spaghetti
2–3 tablespoons basil pesto
1 tablespoon olive oil
1 cup frozen broccoli florets or frozen peas
1 × 425-g tin tuna
100 g pitted or stuffed olives
100 g feta, cut into chunks
salt and freshly ground black pepper

1 Cook spaghetti in a large saucepan of boiling salted water until al dente. Meanwhile, fry the pesto in the oil for a couple of minutes. Add the broccoli, tuna and olives and heat gently until warm.

2 Drain the spaghetti and toss with the tuna mix and feta. Season to taste and serve immediately.

pasta with sardine pesto

Serves: 4 **Preparation:** 5 minutes **Cooking:** 20 minutes

500 g pasta of choice
3 tablespoons olive oil
2 cloves garlic, chopped
8 sardines in oil, drained and chopped
5 anchovy fillets in oil, drained and chopped
juice of 2 lemons
salt and freshly ground black pepper
1 tablespoon chopped fresh parsley, to serve

1 Cook the pasta in a large saucepan of boiling salted water until al dente.

2 Meanwhile, heat the oil and sauté the garlic until it turns golden. Add the sardines and anchovies and cook over a gentle heat until they form a thick paste. Stir in the lemon juice and season to taste.

3 Drain the pasta and mix with the sauce.

4 Serve sprinkled with chopped parsley.

pasta with tuna and mushrooms

Serves: 6 **Preparation:** 5 minutes **Cooking:** 20 minutes

Don't worry if you don't have any mushrooms – this pasta is equally tasty without.

500 g pasta of your choice
⅓ cup olive oil
200 g fresh or tinned mushrooms or champignons
100 g tinned tuna in olive oil, drained
salt and freshly ground black pepper
4 cloves garlic, crushed
1 × 400-g tin tomatoes, coarsely chopped
handful chopped fresh parsley

1 Cook the pasta in a large saucepan of boiling salted water until al dente.

2 Meanwhile, fry the mushrooms in half the oil until soft. Add the tuna and mix, flaking the fish as you go. Season with salt and pepper.

3 In a separate saucepan, fry the garlic in the remaining oil until golden. Add the tomatoes and simmer until the pasta is ready.

4 When the pasta is cooked, drain and return to the saucepan. Pour over the garlicky tomato sauce and mix thoroughly. Then add the tuna mix and parsley and mix again. Serve immediately.

poached salmon in thai coconut broth

Serves: 2–3 **Preparation:** 5 minutes **Cooking:** 15 minutes

2 tablespoons Thai green curry paste
1 tablespoon vegetable oil
1 tablespoon soft brown sugar
1 × 400 ml tin coconut milk
1 cup coconut cream
1 tablespoon fish sauce
2 tablespoons lime juice
4 kaffir lime leaves
1 cup frozen green beans
1 × 415-g tin salmon chunks in brine, drained

1 In a large saucepan, heat the curry paste in the oil for a few minutes. Add all the other ingredients except the salmon and bring to the boil.

2 Add the salmon, cover the saucepan and simmer gently for about 10 minutes.

3 Serve with steamed rice.

spaghetti with crab and saffron

Serves: 4 **Preparation:** 5 minutes **Cooking:** 20 minutes

⅓ cup olive oil
250 g tinned crab meat
3 tablespoons dry white wine
salt and freshly ground black pepper
pinch of saffron powder or threads
400 g spaghetti
chopped fresh parsley, to serve

1 Cook the spaghetti in a large saucepan of boiling salted water until al dente.

2 Meanwhile, heat the oil and gently warm the crab meat. Pour in the white wine and season to taste.

3 Dissolve the saffron in a little warm water and add to the crab mix, stirring until the crab takes on a warm golden colour.

4 Drain the spaghetti and then mix with the crab sauce.

5 Serve immediately, sprinkled with chopped parsley.

steamed ginger fish

Serves: 4 **Preparation:** 7 minutes **Cooking:** 10 minutes

4 frozen fish fillets, defrosted
2 cloves garlic, finely chopped
1 tablespoon crushed ginger (fresh or from a jar)
2 tablespoons soy sauce
1 tablespoon sherry or mirin

1 Place each fillet of fish on a sheet of foil. Strew with the garlic and ginger. Mix together the soy and sherry, then drizzle over the fillets.

2 Wrap the foil parcels loosely, place on a baking tray and cook in a moderate oven for about 15 minutes, or until the flesh is firm but flaky and white.

3 Serve with rice for a refreshing light meal.

tuna empanadas

Serves: 4 **Preparation:** 20 minutes **Cooking:** 45 minutes

½ cup olive oil
675 g potatoes, chopped into small cubes
2 bay leaves
1 onion, chopped
2 cloves garlic, chopped
1 cup frozen peas
1 red capsicum in oil, drained
1 × 425-g tin tuna
½ × 400-g tin tomatoes
cup of white wine
handful of fresh parsley, chopped
salt and freshly ground black pepper
2 teaspoons paprika
500 g frozen shortcrust pastry sheets
1 egg, beaten (or milk)

1 Heat the oil in a large pan and stir-fry the potatoes and bay leaves for 5 minutes. Add the onion and garlic and cook for a further 5 minutes. Add the peas and capsicum and cook for another 5 minutes.

2 Add the tuna, tomatoes, wine and parsley, and simmer until most of the liquid has evaporated. Remove the bay leaves and season with salt, pepper and paprika.

3 Preheat the oven to 200°C. Grease a large shallow baking tin and cut pastry sheets to fit snugly across the bottom. Spread the filling over the base.

4 Moisten the edges of the pastry base and cover the filling with more pastry sheets, pressing the top and bottom edges together with a fork to seal. Brush the top with beaten egg or milk and bake for about 25–30 minutes, or until the top is golden.

5 Cut into squares and serve hot or cold.

tuna pie

Serves: 4 **Preparation:** 15 minutes **Cooking:** 40 minutes

1 tablespoon butter
1 tablespoon plain flour
2 cups milk
1 teaspoon curry powder
juice of ½ a lemon
1 × 425-g tin tuna
100 g tinned or frozen corn kernels
100 g frozen peas

topping
2 cups mashed potato, still hot
1 tablespoon butter
1 tablespoon milk
½ onion, grated
1 egg, lightly beaten
salt and freshly ground black pepper

1 Preheat oven to 180°C.

2 In a saucepan, make a white sauce – mix the butter, flour and milk together and whisk constantly over a medium heat until the sauce is smooth and has thickened. Add the curry powder, lemon juice, tuna, corn and peas. Spoon mixture into a 20-cm ovenproof dish.

3 To make the topping, beat the hot mashed potato with the butter, milk, onion and egg. Season with salt and pepper. Spread mixture over the tuna and bake for 40 minutes or until golden.

variation

Use 500 g of puff pastry instead of the mash. Roll out two thirds of the pastry and use it to line a 20-cm round pie dish. Add the tuna filling and top with the remainder of the pastry. Trim, seal and flute the edges. Brush the top with milk and bake at 200°C for about 40 minutes or until golden brown.

meat and poultry

chicken pizzaiola

Serves: 6 **Preparation:** 10 minutes **Cooking:** 30 minutes

3 tablespoons olive oil
½ onion, finely chopped
3 cloves garlic, chopped
200 ml passata
½ teaspoon dried oregano
1 tablespoon chopped fresh marjoram (optional)
salt and freshly ground black pepper
6 thin chicken fillets, tenderised with a meat mallet
   (beef or pork can be used instead)
2 tablespoons chopped fresh parsley

1 Fry the onion and garlic in the oil until soft and golden. Pour in the passata and add the oregano, marjoram, and salt and pepper. Simmer for 20 minutes.

2 Add the chicken and simmer for another 10 minutes, turning several times.

3 Adjust the seasoning and then sprinkle with parsley.

4 Serve with mashed potato or crusty bread to sop up the juices.

chickpea and chorizo casserole

Serves: 3–4 **Preparation:** 10 minutes **Cooking:** 20 minutes

1 tablespoon olive oil
1 large onion, diced
1 clove garlic, crushed
1 red capsicum in oil, diced (optional)
200 g chorizo sausage, peeled and cut into diagonal slices
480 g tinned chickpeas, drained
1 × 400-g tin tomatoes
1 cup water
salt and freshly ground black pepper

1 Heat oil in a large pan and fry onion until starting to brown. Add the garlic, capsicum and chorizo and sauté until the capsicum is soft and chorizo is sizzling.

2 Add the chickpeas, tomato and water. Season with salt and pepper and simmer for around 20 minutes or until the sauce has thickened.

3 Serve with crusty bread.

fried chicken crispy noodles

Serves: 4 **Preparation:** 15 minutes **Cooking:** 15 minutes

250 g chicken fillets
2 tablespoons cornflour
1 tablespoon sesame oil
1 cup vegetable oil
1 × 225-g packet Chinese crispy noodles
1 tablespoon vegetable oil
½ onion, cut into wedges
1 clove garlic, crushed
sprinkle of dried chilli flakes
1 × 425-g can champignons, drained and sliced
200 g tinned baby corn, drained
1 carrot, peeled and cut into strips
½ cup chopped roasted peanuts or cashews, to serve (optional)

1 Cut chicken into 2-cm strips, then mix with 1 tablespoon of the cornflour and the sesame oil.

2 Heat the vegetable oil in a wok and fry the noodles until crisp. Arrange on individual plates or a serving platter.

3 Heat a tablespoon of oil in the wok and fry the onion wedges, garlic and chilli for a couple of minutes. Add the chicken and fry for 2 minutes. Add the champignons, corn and carrot and continue cooking for 3 minutes.

4 Mix the remaining cornflour with a little cold water to make a paste and add to the wok.

5 Once the sauce has thickened, remove from heat and serve on top of the crispy noodles. Garnish with chopped nuts, if desired.

green pasta and ham

Serves: 6 kids or 4 adults **Preparation:** 10 minutes **Cooking:** 25 minutes

Kids love this dish almost as much as they love the classic Dr Zeuss book.

500 g spinach pasta
3 tablespoons butter
2 tablespoons plain flour
1 cup hot milk
150 g tinned ham or bacon, cut into strips
salt and freshly ground black pepper
150 g parmesan cheese

1 Preheat oven to 220°C.

2 Cook the pasta in a large saucepan of boiling salted water until al dente, drain and set aside.

3 Melt 1 tablespoon of butter in a saucepan, add the flour and stir for 3 minutes. Gradually add the hot milk, whisking continuously. Cook for about 10 minutes or until thickened and smooth.

4 Melt the rest of the butter in a frying pan and cook the ham or bacon. Mix with half the white sauce and the cooked pasta. Season to taste.

5 Place the pasta mix in a large shallow ovenproof dish, pour over the remaining sauce and sprinkle with the parmesan.

6 Bake for about 15–20 minutes or until bubbling and golden on top.

risotto balls

Serves: 2 as a main, or 6 as an appetiser **Preparation:** 15 minutes **Cooking:** 10 minutes

This is a great way of using up any leftover risotto – perhaps as a light lunch for the next day, or as an appetiser.

½ cup olive oil
1 onion, finely chopped
200 g tasty cheese, grated
3 cups cooked risotto
1 egg, beaten
sprinkle of dried chilli flakes
1 clove garlic, finely chopped
zest of 1 lemon
1 teaspoon mixed dried herbs
plain flour, for coating

1 Heat a splash of the oil and cook onion until soft.

2 Mix the cheese with the risotto, add the egg and combine well. Add the onion, chilli, garlic, lemon zest and herbs.

3 Use your hands to mould the mixture into small balls, then roll each ball in flour.

4 Heat the remaining oil in a wok and cook the balls in batches until golden brown. Remove from the oil with a slotted spoon and drain on kitchen paper. Keep the cooked balls warm in the oven while you fry the rest.

risotto with bacon and peas

Serves: 4 **Preparation:** 5 minutes **Cooking:** 20 minutes

½ cup olive oil
1 onion, finely chopped
1 clove garlic, finely chopped
4 rashers bacon, chopped
2 cups risotto rice (Arborio)
1.5 litres vegetable or chicken stock, hot
1 cup frozen peas
handful freshly grated parmesan cheese
bunch of parsley, finely chopped

1 Heat the oil and cook the onion, garlic and bacon until soft. Add the rice and stir for several minutes until the grains are coated with oil.

2 Add a cup of stock and stir until absorbed. Keep adding more liquid as the rice soaks it up. Stir continuously.

3 After about 10 minutes, add the frozen peas. The risotto will be ready after about 20 minutes of cooking, when the rice is soft and creamy and almost all the liquid has been absorbed.

4 Mix in the parmesan and parsley and serve immediately.

alternative risotto flavourings
Instead of bacon and peas, cook the rice as above then add whatever other ingredients you have to hand, for example:
- olives, cheese and red capsicum from a jar
- tinned sardines, plus some passata and black olives
- whatever vegetables are lurking in the crisper drawer, chopped
- fresh herbs and a sprinkling of dried chilli flakes

rosemary chicken casserole

Serves: 6 **Preparation:** 5 minutes **Cooking:** 40–50 minutes

½ cup olive oil
6 chicken breasts, skin removed
3 cloves garlic, finely chopped
3 teaspoons fresh rosemary leaves or 1½ teaspoons dried rosemary
1 × 500-g jar passata or 1 × 400-g tin chopped tomatoes
1 cup chicken stock
salt and freshly ground black pepper

1 Preheat oven to 190°C.

2 Heat 2 tablespoons of the oil in a large frying pan and cook the chicken fillets until well-browned on both sides. Remove chicken from pan and set aside.

3 Heat remaining oil in the frying pan and cook the garlic and rosemary for about 3 minutes.

4 Place chicken fillets, garlic and rosemary in a baking dish, pour over the passata and stock and season with salt and pepper. Cover and bake for 20–30 minutes or until the chicken is cooked through.

5 Serve with rice or crusty bread.

spaghetti with salami

Serves: 4 **Preparation:** 5 minutes **Cooking:** 20 minutes

500 g spaghetti
2 tablespoons olive oil
1 clove garlic, chopped
1 onion, finely chopped
300 g spicy salami or chorizo sausage, sliced
2 tablespoons tomato paste
2 tablespoons capers, rinsed
salt and freshly ground black pepper
freshly grated parmesan cheese or chopped fresh parsley, to serve

1 Cook the spaghetti in a large saucepan of boiling salted water until al dente.

2 In the meantime, heat the olive oil in a pan and gently sauté the garlic and onion. Add the salami and cook until crisp (about 5 minutes). Stir in the tomato paste and capers and cook for another minute or so. Season to taste.

3 Drain the spaghetti and toss with the salami mixture.

4 Garnish with parmesan and/or parsley to serve.

vegetarian

bean salad in pita bread

Serves: 2 **Preparation:** 5 minutes **Cooking**: 5 minutes **Standing:** 20 minutes

1 × 400-g tin red kidney beans
1 large red onion, thinly sliced
½ teaspoon dried chilli flakes
⅓ cup extra virgin olive oil
2 tablespoons white wine vinegar
1 clove garlic, finely chopped
salt and freshly ground black pepper
handful of fresh parsley, chopped
4 frozen pita breads

1 Preheat oven to 160°C.

2 Combine all the ingredients, except for the bread, in a large bowl. Set aside for at least 20 minutes to allow the flavours to develop.

3 Warm the pita breads in the oven until soft, then gently open them up. Spoon the bean salad inside the bread and serve immediately.

cheesy risotto with parsley

Serves: 6 **Preparation:** 5 minutes **Cooking:** 20 minutes

3 tablespoons olive oil
300 g risotto rice (Arborio)
1 cup white wine
1.2 litres vegetable stock, hot (chicken or beef could also be used)
1 tablespoon butter
large bunch parsley, finely chopped
handful freshly grated parmesan cheese
salt and freshly ground black pepper
extra grated parmesan cheese, to serve

1 Heat the olive oil in a large saucepan and add the rice. Stir for several minutes until the grains are coated with oil.

2 Add the white wine and stir until absorbed. Add a cup of stock and stir until absorbed. Keep adding more stock as the rice soaks it up. Stir continuously. Cook for around 20 minutes, until the rice is soft and creamy and almost all the liquid has been absorbed.

3 Stir in the butter, parsley and cheese, and season with salt and pepper.

4 Serve with extra parmesan offered in a bowl.

dhal

Serves: 4 **Preparation:** 5 minutes **Cooking:** 45 minutes

1 tablespoon olive oil
1 onion, finely sliced
1 clove garlic, crushed
1 teaspoon crushed ginger (fresh or from a jar)
½ teaspoon ground cumin
½ teaspoon turmeric
150 g dried red or yellow lentils
½ teaspoon salt
3 cups water

1 In a heavy-based saucepan, heat the oil and fry the onion and garlic until just turning golden. Add the spices and stir for a couple more minutes.

2 Add the lentils, salt and water and simmer for about 45 minutes or until the lentils are very tender. Stir occasionally to prevent sticking, particularly towards the end as the mix reaches the consistency of thick porridge.

3 Serve over rice.

falafels

Serves: 6 **Preparation:** 15 minutes **Cooking:** 10 minutes **Chilling:** 60 minutes

2 × 400-g tins chickpeas, drained
1 onion, finely chopped
1½ cups breadcrumbs
½ cup chopped fresh parsley
½ cup chopped fresh coriander or 2 teaspoons ground coriander
2 teaspoons ground cumin
½ teaspoon salt
2 tablespoons lemon juice
sprinkle of cayenne pepper
vegetable oil for frying
lemon wedges and natural yoghurt, to serve

1 In a food processor, blend all the ingredients until a smooth paste is formed. Form the mixture into balls, adding more breadcrumbs if the mix is too sloppy. Refrigerate for at least 1 hour.

2 Heat the oil in a wok or frying pan and shallow-fry the balls, turning regularly until golden brown all over.

3 Serve with a squeeze of lemon and some yoghurt on the side, or use to fill warmed pita bread.

garlic butterfly pasta

Serves: 4 **Preparation:** 3 minutes **Cooking:** 15 minutes

500 g butterfly pasta
½ cup olive oil
12 cloves garlic, finely chopped
handful chopped parsley, chives or other fresh herbs

1 Cook the pasta in a large saucepan of boiling salted water until al dente.

2 Meanwhile, heat the oil and fry the garlic until it begins to turn golden. Quickly remove the garlic from the oil with a slotted spoon to prevent burning. Reserve the oil and garlic separately.

3 Drain the pasta, then mix with the reserved oil, garlic and herbs.

macaroni cheese

Serves: 4 **Preparation:** 3 minutes **Cooking:** 30 minutes

225 g macaroni
½ cup butter
1 onion, finely chopped
3 tablespoons plain flour
2 cups milk
1 tablespoon wholegrain mustard
1½ cups grated tasty cheese
salt and freshly ground black pepper
½ cup breadcrumbs

1 Preheat oven to 180°C.

2 Cook the macaroni in a large saucepan of boiling salted water until al dente.

3 Meanwhile, melt the butter in a pan and cook the onion gently for about 5 minutes, until soft. Stir in the flour and cook briefly, making sure it doesn't catch. Add the milk and stir constantly until the sauce boils and thickens. Remove from heat and stir in the mustard and most of the cheese. Season to taste.

4 Drain the pasta, then mix it with the sauce and place into a greased ovenproof dish. Sprinkle with breadcrumbs and remaining cheese and bake for about 15 minutes or until the top is golden and bubbling.

megadarra

Serves: 4–6 **Preparation:** 10 minutes **Cooking:** 30 minutes

250 g dried brown lentils
1 tablespoon olive oil
2 large onions, finely chopped
1 bay leaf
1 teaspoon allspice
2 strips lemon zest
salt and freshly ground black pepper
250 g long grain rice
500 ml chicken stock
chopped fresh parsley or grated lemon zest, to serve
natural yoghurt, to serve

1 Rinse the lentils and boil in enough water to cover until just tender (about 25 minutes).

2 Meanwhile, cook the onions in the oil until soft and almost caramelised. Add the bay leaf, allspice and lemon zest, and season to taste with salt and pepper. Add the rice and cover with the chicken stock. Simmer gently until the rice is cooked.

3 Combine the warm rice and drained lentils, and season again to taste. Garnish with parsley or grated lemon zest and serve with natural yoghurt. (Try mixing a little mint sauce and salt and pepper into the yoghurt.)

pappardelle with grilled capsicum, capers and olives

Serves 2–3 **Preparation:** 10 minutes **Cooking:** 20 minutes

½ cup fresh breadcrumbs
225 g pappardelle
3 red capsicums in oil
½ cup olive oil
juice of ½ a lemon
1 dessertspoon capers, rinsed (add more or less, to taste)
4 anchovy fillets in oil, drained and chopped
salt and freshly ground black pepper
1 tablespoon butter
100 g mozzarella cheese, cut into lumps
handful of pitted black olives

1 Toast the breadcrumbs in a frying pan, stirring constantly until they are golden brown. Set aside.

2 Cook the pasta in a large saucepan of boiling salted water until al dente.

3 Meanwhile, rinse the capsicums and cut into strips. Fry with half the olive oil until sizzling. Remove the capsicum strips with a slotted spoon and reserve.

4 Pour any cooking juice from the frying pan into a bowl and mix in the remaining olive oil, lemon juice, capers and anchovies to make the dressing. Season to taste.

5 Drain the pasta and return to the saucepan. Toss with the breadcrumbs, capsicum, mozzarella, olives and dressing.

pasta with crispy parsley

Serves: 4 (or 8 as a side dish) **Preparation:** 5 minutes **Cooking:** 20 minutes

500 g pasta
¼ cup olive oil
2 tablespoons shredded lemon zest
2 tablespoons capers, rinsed
1 cup fresh parsley leaves
1 teaspoon dried chilli flakes
freshly grated parmesan cheese, to serve

1 Cook the pasta in a large saucepan of boiling salted water until al dente. When the pasta is just about ready, heat the oil over a medium heat and gently fry the lemon zest, capers, parsley and chilli until the parsley is crisp.

2 Toss through the drained pasta and serve with parmesan cheese.

pasta with peas in a zesty lemon sauce

Serves: 4 **Preparation:** 10 minutes **Cooking:** 15 minutes

500 g pasta of choice
zest and juice of 2 large lemons
handful of fresh chives, chopped (or 1 tablespoon dried chives)
2 tablespoons chopped fresh parsley
½ cup extra virgin olive oil
salt and freshly ground black pepper
1 cup frozen peas, cooked (or a mix of peas and corn kernels)

1 Cook the pasta in a large saucepan of boiling salted water until al dente.

2 Meanwhile, blend the lemon zest, juice, herbs and a tablespoon of the oil in a food processor. Season to taste with salt and pepper.

3 Drain the pasta and stir in the remaining oil, sauce and peas.

penne with caramelised onion

Serves: 4 **Preparation:** 10 minutes **Cooking:** 20 minutes

100 g butter
2 large onions, finely chopped
2 cloves garlic, finely chopped
salt and freshly ground black pepper
500 g penne
3 eggs, lightly beaten
½ cup freshly grated parmesan cheese

1 Melt the butter in a heavy-based saucepan and cook the onions and garlic until very soft and just beginning to colour. Season to taste and keep warm while the pasta is cooking.

2 Cook the pasta in a large saucepan of boiling salted water until al dente. When it is almost done, return the onions to a low heat and mix in the beaten eggs, stirring for a minute or so until the egg sets.

3 Mix with the drained pasta and parmesan and serve immediately.

penne with chilli, tomato and olives

Serves: 4 **Preparation:** 5 minutes **Cooking:** 20 minutes

400 g penne
1 tablespoon olive oil
1 onion, finely chopped
2 cloves garlic, finely chopped
1 teaspoon dried chilli flakes
2 × 440-g tins tomatoes
1 teaspoon oregano
¼ cup sliced black olives
salt and freshly ground black pepper
freshly grated parmesan cheese, to serve

1 Cook the pasta in a large saucepan of boiling salted water until al dente.

2 Meanwhile, heat the oil over a moderate heat and fry the onion, garlic and chilli until the onion is soft. Add the tomatoes and oregano and crush with a wooden spoon. Simmer until the pasta is ready.

3 Add the olives to the sauce, season to taste, and toss with the drained pasta.

4 Serve with parmesan on the side.

refried bean patties

Serves: 4 **Preparation:** 10 minutes **Cooking:** 10 minutes

2 tablespoon olive oil
2 onions, finely chopped
1 clove garlic, finely chopped
½ cup tomato purée
½ teaspoon cayenne pepper
2 cups tinned beans (red kidney, pinto, borlotti, etc.)
4 tablespoons plain flour or breadcrumbs
vegetable oil for frying

1 Sauté the onions and garlic in the olive oil until golden. Add the tomato purée and cayenne pepper. Drop the beans in by spoonfuls, mashing and stirring as you go.

2 When the mixture is dry and firm, take off the heat and let cool.

3 Shape mixture into patties with wet hands, coat in flour and fry on both sides until golden brown.

4 Serve immediately.

risotto with dried mushrooms

Serves: 4 **Preparation:** 10 minutes **Cooking:** 20 minutes **Standing:** 60 minutes

50 g dried mushrooms
1 tablespoon olive oil
1 onion, finely chopped
1 clove garlic, finely chopped
3 cups risotto rice (Arborio)
½ teaspoon dried thyme
1.2 litres chicken stock, hot
salt and freshly ground black pepper
1 cup freshly grated parmesan cheese

1 Soak mushrooms in hot water for a least an hour.

2 Cook the onion and garlic in the olive oil until softened. Add the rice and stir for several minutes until the grains are coated with oil. Add the drained mushrooms, thyme and a cup of stock and stir well.

3 Keep adding more liquid as the rice soaks it up. Stir continuously. Cook for around 20 minutes, until the rice is soft and creamy and almost all the liquid has been absorbed.

4 Remove from the heat, season to taste and stir in the parmesan.

spaghetti with artichokes

Serves: 4 **Preparation:** 5 minutes **Cooking:** 20 minutes

500 g spaghetti
2 tablespoons olive oil
1 clove garlic, chopped
1 onion, finely chopped
350 g artichoke hearts in oil, drained and chopped
pinch of dried chilli flakes
pinch of dried oregano or marjoram
6 tablespoons black olive paste (tapenade)
salt and freshly ground black pepper
chopped fresh parsley, to serve
freshly grated parmesan cheese, to serve

1 Cook the spaghetti in a large saucepan of boiling salted water until al dente.

2 Meanwhile, gently sauté the garlic and onion in the olive oil. Add the artichokes, chilli and oregano.

3 Drain the spaghetti and toss with the olive paste, then the artichoke mixture.

4 Garnish with parsley and parmesan to serve.

spaghetti with sun-dried tomatoes

Serves: 4 **Preparation:** 5 minutes **Cooking:** 20 minutes

500 g spaghetti
⅓ cup olive oil
1 small onion, finely chopped
250 g sun-dried tomatoes
300 g tinned tomatoes
salt and freshly ground black pepper
freshly grated parmesan cheese, to serve

1 Cook the spaghetti in a large saucepan of boiling salted water until al dente.

2 Meanwhile, heat the oil and fry the onion until soft. Add the sun-dried tomatoes and cook for 5 minutes, then add the tinned tomatoes.

3 Cook over a high heat until the sauce has thickened. Season to taste, bearing in mind that sun-dried tomatoes are often quite salty.

4 Drain the pasta and stir through the sauce.

5 Serve with freshly grated parmesan cheese.

spanish tortilla

Serves: 2 **Preparation:** 10 minutes **Cooking:** 20 minutes

⅓ cup olive oil
350 g potatoes, peeled and sliced
1 onion, thinly sliced
5 eggs, beaten
salt
1 large baguette, to serve (optional)
mayonnaise, to serve (optional)

1 Heat the oil in a frying pan and stir-fry the potato and onion slices over a high heat for several minutes. Reduce the heat, cover and cook until the potatoes are soft and the onions are golden (about 10 minutes). Stir occasionally to prevent sticking.

2 Beat the eggs with salt to taste and pour them into the pan over the potato and onion mix. After a couple of minutes, lift the edge of the tortilla and check the colour. When the bottom is set and golden brow, place the pan under the grill until the top is also golden. Allow to cool.

3 For a tasty light meal for two, cut a baguette in half, slice lengthwise and fill with chunks of tortilla and a generous dollop of mayonnaise.

spinach frittata

Serves: 4 **Preparation:** 10 minutes **Cooking:** 10 minutes

⅓ cup olive oil
2 onions, finely chopped
250 g frozen spinach, cooked, drained and chopped
6 eggs, beaten
150 g parmesan cheese, freshly grated
salt and freshly ground black pepper

1 Fry the onions and spinach in 2 tablespoons of the oil until onion is soft.

2 Mix the onion and spinach mixture with the beaten eggs, then add the cheese.
Season to taste.

3 Heat the remaining oil in a wide frying pan until very hot. Pour in the egg mixture
and tilt the pan so that it spreads evenly across the base. Cook until the underside
is brown and firm.

4 Carefully flip the frittata onto a plate, then slide back into the pan to cook the other side.
Alternatively, you can leave the frittata in the pan and cook the top in the oven or under
the grill until golden brown.

5 Serve hot or cold, cut into wedges.

vegetable curry in a flash

Serves: 4 **Preparation:** 5 minutes **Cooking:** 25 minutes

2 tablespoons vegetable oil
1 onion, chopped
1 clove garlic, crushed
1½ tablespoons curry powder
1 × 400-g tin crushed tomatoes (or use passata)
2 × 300-g tins chickpeas, drained
3 medium potatoes, peeled and chopped
2 carrots, peeled and chopped
½ cup frozen peas
natural yoghurt and Indian relishes, to serve

1 Heat oil in a large saucepan and cook onion, garlic and curry powder until the onion is soft and golden.

2 Add the rest of the ingredients. Cover and simmer for around 30 minutes, or until the potato is soft (stir occasionally to prevent burning).

3 Serve with natural yoghurt and Indian relishes on the side.

lemon and spinach pilaf

side dishes and salads

burghul pilaf

Serves: 4–6 **Preparation:** 3 minutes **Cooking:** 10 minutes

Burghul makes an excellent alternative to rice or couscous. You can dress it up by stirring in some herbs, toasted pine nuts or almonds, sultanas, diced grilled capsicum, sautéed onion, cooked chickpeas or small cubes of tasty cheese – or a combination of these.

500 g burghul
1 litre water or stock
salt and freshly ground black pepper
100 g butter

1 Rinse the burghul well, then put into a saucepan with the liquid. Season to taste. Cook for 10 minutes or until the liquid has been absorbed and the grains are tender.

2 Stir in the butter, take off the heat and leave for 20 minutes before serving to allow the grains to swell.

cannellini bean salad

Serves: 4–6 **Preparation:** 10 minutes **Cooking:** 2 minutes **Standing:** 20 minutes

200 g frozen green beans
2 × 400-g tins cannellini beans, drained
1 cup sun-dried tomatoes in oil, drained
1 teaspoon paprika
½ cup fresh mint leaves, chopped
2 tablespoons extra virgin olive oil
juice of 1 lemon
salt and freshly ground black pepper

1 Microwave or steam the beans until just tender but still very green. Allow to cool and then slice.

2 In a salad bowl, combine the green beans with all the other ingredients. Toss and allow to stand for at least 20 minutes before serving, to allow the flavours to develop.

couscous salad with root vegetables

Serves: 4 **Preparation:** 15 minutes **Cooking:** 45 minutes **Standing:** 10 minutes

500 g chopped root vegetables (pumpkin, carrot, potato or sweet potato) and
   any other vegetables you have in the fridge (capsicum, corn, zucchini, etc.)
   – use tinned red kidney or borlotti beans if you don't have any fresh vegetables
2 cups large (pearl) couscous
2½ cups stock
salt and freshly ground black pepper

dressing
¼ cup extra virgin olive oil
½ teaspoon chilli or harissa paste
¼ cup lemon juice
1 tablespoon honey
¼ cup finely chopped fresh mint or parsley

1 Preheat oven to 200°C. Roast root vegetables for about 35 minutes (add vegetables such as capsicum, corn and zucchini after about 20 minutes). Toss vegetables once or twice during cooking.

2 Bring stock to the boil and add couscous. Simmer, covered, for 10 minutes until liquid is absorbed and couscous is tender. Remove from heat and let stand, covered, for 10 minutes. Stir and season to taste.

3 Mix all dressing ingredients together and toss with the couscous and vegetables. Serve warm or cold.

variation
You can use ordinary couscous instead of large couscous. Place couscous in a large bowl and pour over boiling stock. Cover and let stand until the grains are fluffy and the liquid has been absorbed. Stir and season to taste before mixing in the dressing and roasted vegetables.

fried rice

Serves: 4 **Preparation:** 10 minutes **Cooking:** 7 minutes

1 cup rice
2 tablespoons vegetable oil
2 eggs, beaten
4 bacon rashers
1 onion, finely chopped
1 clove garlic, crushed
1 tablespoon crushed ginger (fresh or from a jar)
100 g prawns (tinned, or frozen and defrosted)
1 × 425-g can baby corn, drained and sliced
½ cup frozen peas, thawed
1 tablespoon soy sauce
pinch five-spice powder

1 Cook rice in a large saucepan of boiling salted water. Leave to cool.

2 Heat 1 tablespoon of vegetable oil in a wok or frying pan, then fry the egg to make a thin omelette. Remove from pan, roll and cut into thin slivers.

3 Stir-fry bacon and onion in remaining oil until cooked, then add the garlic and ginger and cook for a couple of minutes longer.

4 Add the rice, omelette and remaining ingredients to the pan and stir-fry until heated through.

garlic chickpeas

Serves: 4–6 **Preparation:** 5 minutes **Standing:** 30 minutes

2 × 400-g tins chickpeas, drained
⅓ cup lemon juice
2 cloves garlic, crushed
½ cup finely chopped fresh parsley
¼ cup olive oil
⅓ cup grated parmesan cheese
salt and freshly ground black pepper to taste

1 Mix all ingredients together and let stand for at least 30 minutes before serving, to allow the flavours to develop.

golden onion couscous

Serves: 4 **Preparation:** 5 minutes **Cooking:** 10 minutes

⅓ cup olive oil
4 onions, sliced
2 cups couscous
2½ cups stock, boiling
2 tablespoons wholegrain mustard
1 tablespoon lemon juice
salt and freshly ground black pepper

1 Heat two tablespoons of the oil and cook the onion for about 10 minutes, stirring occasionally, until golden.

2 Meanwhile, place couscous in a large bowl and pour over the boiling stock. Cover and let stand until the grains are fluffy and the liquid has been absorbed.

3 In a small bowl, combine the remaining oil, mustard and lemon juice. Season to taste. Toss the dressing with the couscous and onions. Serve immediately.

green bean and egg salad

Serves: 4–6 **Preparation:** 5 minutes **Cooking:** 5 minutes

225 g frozen green beans
1 red onion, finely diced
3 eggs, hardboiled and finely chopped
⅔ cup extra virgin olive oil
3 teaspoons balsamic vinegar
salt and freshly ground black pepper

1 Microwave or steam the beans until just tender but still very green. Drain and cool, then place in a serving dish. Scatter the onion and egg over the top.

2 Mix the oil and vinegar together and season to taste.

3 Dress the salad and toss well before serving.

indian spiced potato patties (aloo kofta)

Serves: 6–8 **Preparation:** 20 minutes **Cooking:** 30 minutes

675 g potatoes, peeled
3 tablespoons vegetable oil
pinch of cinnamon
½ teaspoon curry powder
¼ teaspoon cayenne
½ teaspoon turmeric
salt and freshly ground black pepper
2 eggs, beaten
1 small onion, diced
pinch of dried chilli flakes
1 cup plain flour
vegetable oil for frying
natural yoghurt and/or mango or lime chutney, to serve

1 Boil the potatoes and once cooked mash them with the oil and spices.

2 Add the eggs, onion and chilli to the mix and combine well. Add half the flour and mix to a stiff dough.

3 Use the rest of the flour to dust a work surface. With floured hands, make around 12 sausage-shaped patties. Make sure they are well coated with flour so that they hold together during cooking.

4 Heat the frying oil in a large pan and cook the koftas in batches. Fry on both sides until golden, then drain on kitchen paper.

5 Serve hot with yoghurt or chutney.

italian chicken salad

Serves: 2–3 (4–6 as a side dish) **Preparation:** 5 minutes **Cooking:** 15–20 minutes
(less if using precooked vegetables and meat)

2 chicken breasts, cooked and cubed (or use leftover cooked chicken)
2 potatoes, boiled and cubed
2 carrots, boiled and cubed
150 g frozen green beans, cooked and chopped into short lengths
1 cup frozen peas, cooked
100 g tinned whole baby beets
½ cup mayonnaise
2 tablespoons lemon juice
salt and freshly ground black pepper

1 In a large serving dish, mix the vegetables and chicken together. Add the mayonnaise and lemon juice and season to taste. Toss well to combine.

lemon and spinach pilaf

Serves: 4 **Preparation:** 5 minutes **Cooking:** 15 minutes

1½ cups basmati rice
2 cups chicken or vegetable stock
1 tablespoon shredded lemon zest
1 cup frozen spinach, cooked and shredded
salt and freshly ground black pepper

1 Rinse the rice and place into a saucepan with the stock and lemon zest. Cook over a medium heat for about 10 minutes or until the stock has almost all been absorbed. Remove from heat.

2 Add the cooked spinach, cover and leave for 5 minutes. Season to taste and serve.

mollie's vinaigrette

Preparation: 1 minute

1 part extra-virgin olive oil
1 part balsamic vinegar
1 part honey
freshly ground black pepper

1 Place oil, vinegar and honey into a screw-top jar with some black pepper. Shake vigorously until well-combined.

patatas bravas

Serves: 8 **Preparation:** 10 minutes **Cooking:** 40 minutes

1.5 kg white potatoes
½ cup olive oil
1 onion, chopped
3 cloves garlic, chopped
¼ teaspoon chilli powder
2 teaspoons paprika
⅓ cup dry white wine
1 × 400-g tin diced tomatoes
1 teaspoon fresh or dried oregano
salt and freshly ground black pepper
finely chopped fresh parsley, to serve

1 Preheat oven to 200°C.

2 Fill a large saucepan with water, add the potatoes and bring to the boil. Cook until just firm. Drain and cool.

3 Pour half the oil into a large roasting pan and heat in the oven for about 5 minutes, until the oil is hot. Add the potatoes to the pan and turn to coat in oil. Roast for about 15–20 minutes, until crisp and tender.

4 In the meantime, gently heat the remaining oil in a saucepan. Add the onion and cook until soft, then add the garlic, chilli and paprika. Cook for another minute while stirring continuously. Add the wine and bring to the boil.

5 When the liquid has reduced by half, add the tomatoes and oregano. Simmer for 20 minutes until the sauce has thickened.

6 Blend the sauce in a food processor until smooth, and season with salt and pepper.

7 Transfer the potatoes to a serving bowl, spoon over the sauce and garnish with parsley.

polenta

Serves: 4 **Preparation:** 1 minute **Cooking:** 10 minutes

¾ cup polenta (5 minute or instant variety)
4 cups water
2 teaspoons salt
1 tablespoon butter
freshly ground black pepper

1 Mix the polenta, water and salt in a microwave-proof bowl and cook on high for 6 minutes. Stir, then cook for another 3 minutes, until the polenta becomes thick and gluggy. (For a stovetop method, see Polenta Wedges, opposite.)

2 Stir in the butter and season generously with black pepper.

3 Serve as a side dish as is, or add parmesan cheese, pesto, blue cheese, tapenade or your flavouring of choice and eat as a light meal.

polenta wedges

Serves: 4 **Preparation:** 1 minute **Cooking:** 10 minutes **Standing:** 20 minutes

750 ml water
1 dessertspoon salt
200 g polenta (5 minute or instant variety)
2 tablespoons olive oil
25 g parmesan cheese, freshly grated
salt and freshly ground black pepper

1 Bring the water to boil in a large saucepan. Add the salt, then add the polenta in a steady stream, stirring continuously. Keep stirring for about 7 minutes, or until the polenta is thick like porridge. (For a microwave method, see Polenta, opposite.)

2 Add the remaining ingredients and mix well.

3 Pour the mix onto a clean chopping board or roasting dish and level the surface. Allow to cool for about 20 minutes.

4 Slice into squares and grill or pan fry as an accompaniment to a salad or main meal. For an appetiser or snack, dress the wedges with your choice of topping (such as passata and grated tasty cheese, or ham and gorgonzola), and bake until golden and bubbling.

potato and spinach croquettes

Makes: 15 **Preparation:** 10 minutes **Cooking:** 30 minutes

500 g floury potatoes
1 tablespoon butter
pinch of nutmeg
salt and freshly ground pepper
½ cup freshly grated parmesan cheese
½ cup frozen spinach, cooked, drained and finely chopped
flour, for dusting work surface
3 tablespoons plain flour
3 eggs, beaten
1 tablespoon vegetable oil
150 g dried breadcrumbs
vegetable oil for frying

1 Boil and mash the potatoes.

2 Mix the mashed potato with the butter and nutmeg and season to taste with salt and pepper. Add the parmesan and well-drained spinach and mix thoroughly. (The mixture must not be too wet or the croquettes will fall apart during cooking).

3 On a floured surface, roll handfuls of the potato mixture into about 15 sausage shapes.

4 Place the plain flour on a flat plate, combine the eggs with the oil in a bowl, and place the breadcrumbs on another large flat plate.

5 Gently roll each croquette in flour, dip in the egg mix, then roll in the breadcrumbs. You may need to repeat this step if the coating is uneven.

6 Heat some vegetable oil in a large frying pan or deep fryer and fry the croquettes in batches until golden brown. Drain on kitchen paper and serve immediately.

potatoes niçoise

Serves: 4 **Preparation:** 10 minutes **Cooking:** 20–30 minutes

250 g potatoes
2 fresh tomatoes, cut into chunks (or use
  ½ cup sun-dried tomatoes in oil)
8 anchovy fillets in oil, drained
90 g frozen broad beans, cooked
½ onion, finely chopped
1 tablespoon capers, rinsed
2 eggs, hardboiled and chopped
chopped fresh chives or parsley, to serve

dressing
1 tablespoon mayonnaise
1 tablespoon extra virgin olive oil
good squeeze lemon juice
salt and freshly ground black pepper

1 Boil the potatoes, allow to cool, then chop into chunks.

2 Gently mix the potatoes, tomatoes, anchovies, beans, onion, capers and egg together in a serving bowl.

3 Place all dressing ingredients into a screw-top jar and shake well.

4 Gently toss the dressing through the salad.

5 Garnish with chopped chives or parsley, if you have some.

red onion relish

Makes: 1 cup **Preparation:** 3 minutes **Cooking:** 10 minutes

2 tablespoons olive oil
3 onions, sliced finely
½ teaspoon chopped fresh thyme
1 teaspoon wholegrain mustard

1 Heat olive oil in a pan and gently fry the onion, thyme and wholegrain mustard until golden.

2 Serve with cold meat and salad in a sandwich, on a baked potato, or as an accompaniment to a main meal.

rice every which way

Serves: 4 **Preparation:** 1 minute **Cooking:** 10–12 minutes

Even if you have nothing much left in your cupboard except a bag of rice, you can whip up a spectacular side dish or light meal with just a few extra ingredients you find lurking in the fridge.

1 cup long grain white rice
1 teaspoon salt

1 Place rice and salt into a saucepan, and cover with enough water to reach up to the first knuckle of your index finger when the tip of your finger is resting on top of the rice (around 400 ml). Bring to the boil, then turn the heat down to a simmer and cover with a lid. Cook for around 10 minutes.

2 Lift the lid and check to see how the rice is looking. The water should have been absorbed and the rice should be fluffy. Taste a few grains to see if it is tender. If the rice is ready, remove from heat, replace the lid and let sit for a few minutes.

3 Stir through whatever additions you have to hand.

suggestions to stir into rice
- Tinned champignons, sautéed in butter with a little ground coriander
- A tin of lentils, drained and warmed through with a teaspoon of butter
- Black olive paste and sun-dried tomatoes
- Bacon, cooked till crisp, and parmesan cheese
- Basil pesto from a jar
- Spicy harissa paste
- Toasted almonds or pine nuts and raisins
- Frozen spinach, shredded and cooked in butter

salmon and olive pasta salad

Serves: 4 **Preparation:** 5 minutes **Cooking:** 10–12 minutes

375 g shell or spiral pasta
2 × 415-g tins salmon, drained
1 large red onion, finely chopped
350 g small gherkins, chopped
1 tablespoon olives, chopped
handful fresh parsley, finely chopped

dressing
½ cup extra virgin olive oil
½ cup lemon juice
1 tablespoon wholegrain mustard
1 tablespoon honey

1 Cook the pasta in a large saucepan of boiling salted water until al dente and drain. Remove bones from the salmon and flake the flesh with a fork.

2 Gently mix salmon and pasta with the onion, gherkins, olives and parsley.

3 Place all dressing ingredients into a screw-top jar and shake well.

4 To serve, pour dressing over the salad and toss gently.

sesame chickpea cannonballs

Serves: 4 **Preparation:** 10 minutes **Cooking:** 10 minutes

1 × 400-g tin chickpeas, drained
2 tablespoons sesame oil
salt and freshly ground black pepper
2 eggs, beaten
125 g sesame seeds
vegetable oil for frying
natural yoghurt and/or tomato or sweet chilli relish, to serve

1 Purée the chickpeas and sesame oil in a food processor until smooth, then season to taste with salt and pepper.

2 Roll the mixture into small balls, dip in the beaten egg and roll in the sesame seeds.

3 Heat the oil until a cube of bread sizzles and turns brown in 30 seconds, then fry the balls in batches until golden brown. Drain on kitchen paper.

4 Serve immediately with yoghurt or relish.

spicy chickpeas

Serves: 6 **Preparation:** 5 minutes **Cooking:** 10 minutes

2 × 400-g tins chickpeas, drained
⅓ cup passata
3 cloves garlic, finely chopped
1 bay leaf
pinch of cinnamon
4 cloves
1 teaspoon ground cumin
1 teaspoon ground coriander
1 teaspoon cayenne pepper
1 teaspoon turmeric
salt and freshly ground black pepper
2 tablespoons olive oil
2 tablespoons white wine vinegar
juice of ½ a lemon
handful chopped fresh parsley or coriander, to serve

1 Place all the ingredients into a large saucepan, cover and simmer gently for about 10 minutes. Remove the lid and continue cooking until most of the liquid has evaporated.

2 Remove the bay leaf and cloves and stir in the parsley or coriander.

3 Serve cold or hot.

tuna and borlotti bean salad

Serves: 4 **Preparation:** 5 minutes **Standing:** 20 minutes

1 × 400-g tin borlotti beans (or other beans), drained and rinsed
1 × 425-g tin tun, flaked
1 large onion, sliced thinly
2 tablespoons chopped fresh parsley

dressing
½ cup olive oil
1 tablespoon white wine vinegar
salt and freshly ground black pepper

1 Mix the beans with the tuna in a salad bowl. Add onion and parsley, and combine well.

2 To make the dressing, place the oil, vinegar and seasoning in a screw-top jar and shake well. Pour over the salad and toss.

3 Let stand for at least 20 minutes before serving.

coconut lemon rissoto

desserts

apricot and almond pudding

Serves: 4–6 **Preparation:** 10 minutes **Cooking:** 60 minutes

175 g unsalted butter, softened
175 g castor sugar
175 g ground almonds
3 eggs, separated
1 teaspoon vanilla extract
8 tinned apricot halves

1 Preheat oven to 150°C. Grease a 5-cm deep, 20-cm square baking dish.

2 Cream the butter with the sugar, then add the ground almonds and mix well. Add the beaten egg yolks and vanilla.

3 In a separate bowl, whisk the egg whites until stiff, then fold into the almond mixture. Spoon into the prepared dish and arrange apricot halves on top.

4 Bake for 30 minutes, then turn oven temperature up to 180°C. Cook for a further 30 minutes or until the top is golden and a skewer inserted into the middle comes out clean.

5 Serve warm with ice-cream.

berry surprise pie

Serves: 4–6 **Preparation:** 10 minutes **Cooking:** 30 minutes

500 g frozen puff pastry
700 g frozen berries
1 egg
castor sugar, for sprinkling
icing sugar, for dusting

1 Preheat oven to 200°C and grease a baking tray.

2 Roll out the puff pastry on a floured surface to make a 30-cm round and transfer to the baking tray.

3 Pile the berries into the centre of the pastry, leaving a handful aside for decoration. Beat the egg with a little water and brush the outer rim of the pastry.

4 Bring the pastry edge towards the middle, leaving a hole in the centre. Pleat and fold the pastry over the fruit to create a rim. Brush top with the rest of the egg mix and sprinkle with castor sugar.

5 Bake for 30 minutes or until the pastry is puffed and golden.

6 Dust with icing sugar, sprinkle the reserved berries over the top, and serve warm with cream or ice-cream.

blueberry pancakes

Serves: 4–6 **Preparation:** 7 minutes **Cooking:** 10 minutes

2 eggs
½ cup milk
¼ cup castor sugar
1 teaspoon vanilla extract
1 cup self-raising flour
2 cups frozen blueberries, defrosted
butter, for frying
maple syrup, to serve

1 Whisk together eggs, milk, sugar, vanilla and sifted flour, then stir in the blueberries. Place batter in a jug for easy pouring.

2 Heat some butter in a frying pan until it is foaming, then add about ¼ cup of batter to the pan. Depending on the size of your pan, you may have room for three or four pancakes at a time.

3 Cook pancakes for about 2 minutes or until bubbles appear on the surface. Flip over and cook on the other side for about a minute, until golden. Stack pancakes on a plate and keep warm. Cook the remaining batter, adding more butter to the pan between batches.

4 Serve warm with maple syrup.

cheat's trifle

Serves: 4 **Preparation:** 15 minutes **Freezing:** 15 minutes

10 sponge fingers or a stale sponge cake, broken into 3-cm pieces
1 cup sweet white wine or liqueur of your choice
2 cups frozen berries or tinned fruit
2 tablespoons castor sugar
2 cups vanilla ice-cream, slightly softened

1 Place half the sponge pieces into a pretty serving dish (or use individual dishes or glasses). Pour over half the liqueur to saturate the sponge. Scatter over a third of the berries and sprinkle with half the sugar. Put half the ice-cream on top of the berries and smooth out to make an even layer.

2 Repeat this process with the remaining ingredients, finishing with a third of the berries on top.

3 This dessert should be placed in the freezer for at least 15 minutes once prepared, but should be removed at least 15 minutes before serving.

variation
If you don't have any frozen or tinned berries, you can use tinned apricots or peaches instead (drained well). If using dried fruit (such as apricots), simply cover in boiling water and leave to soak for 30 minutes. Cool and drain before use.

cinnamon crumble

Serves: 4 **Preparation:** 10 minutes **Cooking:** 30 minutes

500 g sliced fruit (fresh, tinned or frozen)
¾ cup rolled oats
1 cup soft brown sugar
½ cup plain flour
100 g butter, softened
2 teaspoons cinnamon
½ cup crushed unsalted nuts (almonds, walnuts etc.), optional

1 Preheat oven to 180°C and lightly grease a pie or casserole dish.

2 Place the fruit into the dish. Sprinkle with some extra sugar if using fresh fruit such as apples or peaches.

3 In a bowl, use your fingers to mix together the other ingredients until the mixture forms rough crumbs.

4 Spread over the fruit and bake for 30 minutes.

coconut lemon risotto

Serves: 4–6 **Preparation:** 2 minutes **Cooking:** 40 minutes

3 cups coconut milk
zest of 1 lemon, cut into strips
2 tablespoons butter
1 cup risotto rice (Arborio)
½ cup sugar
stewed or fresh fruit, to serve

1 Preheat oven to 190°C and lightly grease a shallow heatproof dish.

2 Place the coconut milk, lemon zest and butter in a saucepan and heat until hot but not boiling.

3 Pour the coconut milk mixture into the baking dish and add the rice and sugar. Stir and cover tightly with a lid or foil. Bake for 30 minutes or until creamy and only a little moist. Stir and remove the lemon zest.

4 Serve hot with some stewed or fresh fruit.

frozen berry bombe

Serves: 4 **Preparation:** 10 minutes **Freezing:** 60 minutes

300 g good quality vanilla ice-cream, softened
3 tablespoons honey
½ cup slivered almonds
200 g frozen berries

1 Using a hand-held beater, mix the ice-cream, honey and almonds until combined. Fold in berries, taking care not to squash them.

2 Transfer to a freezer-proof container, cover with a lid or plastic film and freeze until firm (at least an hour).

golden bread and butter pudding

Serves: 4 **Preparation:** 10 minutes **Cooking:** 25 minutes

4 slices white bread
3 tablespoons golden syrup
3 eggs, beaten
1½ cups cream
1 cup milk
1 teaspoon vanilla extract
3 tablespoons castor sugar
½ cup sultanas
cinnamon or nutmeg, for sprinkling

1 Preheat the oven to 160°C and grease a pie dish.

2 Spread the bread slices with golden syrup and cut each into four triangles. Arrange in an overlapping pattern in the pie dish.

3 Whisk together the eggs, cream, milk, vanilla and castor sugar. Pour mixture over the bread, then sprinkle with the sultanas and cinnamon.

4 Bake for 25 minutes or until the custard has set.

5 Serve immediately, with ice-cream.

summer pudding

Serves: 4–6 **Preparation:** 10 minutes **Chilling:** 10 hours

8 slices bread, crusts removed
750 g frozen mixed berries, defrosted
125 g castor sugar

1 Line a 900-ml pudding basin with the bread, making sure the pieces fit together snugly. Save a few pieces for covering the top of the basin.

2 Bring the fruit and sugar to the boil in a large saucepan, then simmer for a few minutes until the sugar has dissolved and the juices start running freely.

3 Spoon the fruit into the lined basin, keeping a little juice in reserve. Cover the top with the remaining bread.

4 Place a plate or saucer on top of the pudding and weigh down with a heavy jar or tin. Refrigerate for 10 hours, or until set.

5 To serve, remove the plate from the top of the pudding and replace with an inverted serving plate. Turn upside down to release the pudding onto the serving plate. Pour the reserved juice over any bread that has not been stained by the filling.

upside down fruit pie

Serves: 4 **Preparation:** 10 minutes **Cooking:** 30 minutes **Chilling:** 20 minutes

1 cup castor sugar
¼ cup water
1 tablespoon red-wine vinegar
1 × 400-g tin fruit (apricots, peaches, pears, etc.), drained
splash of brandy or other liqueur
1 sheet frozen puff or shortcrust pastry
1 egg yolk
1 tablespoon milk

1 Preheat the oven to 200°C and grease a 25-cm pie dish.

2 Heat sugar and water in a saucepan until sugar has dissolved. Boil until the syrup turns golden, then very carefully add the vinegar (it will spit). Stir until smooth, then pour into the pie dish, coating the base.

3 Toss the fruit with the brandy and place in the dish. Cover the fruit with the pastry, pressing the pastry firmly against the edges of the pie dish. Refrigerate for 20 minutes.

4 Mix the egg and milk together and brush over the pastry. Bake for around 30 minutes or until the top is brown. Run a knife around the edge of the pie dish and carefully turn the pie over onto a serving plate.

5 Serve hot, with cream or ice-cream.

all-purpose butter cake

baking

all-purpose butter cake

Serves: 8 **Preparation:** 10 minutes **Cooking:** 50 minutes

250 g butter, softened
1 cup castor sugar
pinch of salt
3 eggs
1 teaspoon vanilla extract
2 cups self-raising flour
¼ cup milk, at room temperature

1 Preheat oven to 180°C and grease a 25-cm cake tin.

2 Cream the butter, sugar and salt until white and fluffy. Add the eggs one at a time, beating between each addition. Beat in the vanilla extract.

3 Gently fold in the sifted flour in several lots, alternating with the milk, keeping the mix as light as possible.

4 Pour mixture into prepared tin and bake for 50 minutes or until a skewer inserted into the middle comes out clean.

5 Remove from oven and cool in the tin for 10 minutes before turing out onto a wire rack to cool completely.

variation

Just by adding an extra ingredient, you can give this cake a whole new flavour. Try adding some lemon zest for a lemony cake, a tablespoon of cocoa for a chocolate cake, chopped dried apricots for an apricot cake, or some choc chips for a choc-chip cake. This versatile batter can also be baked in cupcake papers or greased muffin tins.

For a simple icing, add enough water to 2 cups icing sugar to make a smooth icing. Use lemon or orange juice instead of water for lemon or orange icing, or add 1 tablespoon cocoa to the icing sugar for chocolate icing.

anzac biscuits

Makes: about 30 **Preparation:** 10 minutes **Cooking:** 12 minutes

100 g butter
2 tablespoons boiling water
1 teaspoon bicarbonate of soda
2 tablespoons golden syrup
2 cups rolled oats
1 cup sugar
¾ cup desiccated coconut
1 cup plain flour

1 Preheat oven to 190°C and grease a couple of baking trays.

2 Melt the butter in the microwave or in a small saucepan, then add the boiling water, bicarbonate of soda and golden syrup. Mix well.

3 In a separate bowl, mix the oats, sugar, coconut and sifted flour. Add the syrup mixture and mix well.

4 Drop spoonfuls of mixture onto the trays and cook for 10–12 minutes until golden.

chocolate cupcakes

Makes: 12 **Preparation:** 10 minutes **Cooking:** 20 minutes

125 g butter, softened
¾ cup sugar
1 teaspoon vanilla extract
2 eggs
1¼ cups self-raising flour
¼ cup cocoa
¼ cup milk

1 Preheat oven to 180°C and lightly grease and flour a muffin tray (or line with cupcake papers).

2 Cream butter, sugar and vanilla. Beat in the eggs one at a time. Fold in the sifted flour and cocoa in several lots, alternating with the milk, to form a smooth batter.

3 Spoon the mix into the prepared tray. Bake for 20 minutes or until a skewer inserted comes out clean.

4 Remove cupcakes from the tin and cool on a wire rack before decorating.

suggested decorations

Decorate cupcakes with pink or chocolate icing. Then sprinkle with hundreds and thousands, or top with a sugar flower.

To make pink icing, mix a teaspoon of melted butter into 2 cups sifted icing sugar. Add enough water to make a smooth icing. Add a few drops pink food colouring and stir until you have an even colour.

To make chocolate icing, follow the same method, but sift 1 tablespoon cocoa into the icing sugar before you add the butter and omit the food colouring.

damper

Makes: 1 loaf **Preparation:** 5 minutes **Cooking:** 25 minutes

3 cups self-raising flour
½ teaspoon salt
4 tablespoons butter, cold
1½ cups milk, water or a mix of both

1 Preheat the oven to 200°C and grease a baking tray.

2 Sift flour and salt into a bowl. Add butter and rub in with your fingertips until it resembles breadcrumbs. Add the liquid and knead to a soft dough.

3 Place the dough onto a floured board and shape into a round loaf. Brush with a little extra milk and bake for 20–25 minutes or until the loaf sounds hollow when tapped.

variation

For a savoury damper, perhaps to accompany soup, add some finely chopped onion, cooked bacon or grated tasty cheese – either add to the dough before you add the liquid, or strew across the top of the dough before baking. Poppy or sesame seeds could also be used.

A sweet loaf can be made by omitting the salt and mixing in ½ cup dried fruit, a tablespoon of sugar and a teaspoon of mixed spice.

muffins

Makes: 12 large muffins **Preparation:** 5 minutes **Cooking:** 20 minutes

220 g self-raising flour
½ cup sugar
¾ cup milk
1 egg
¾ cup vegetable oil
flavourings of your choice

1 Preheat oven to 180°C and grease a muffin tray.

2 Sift the flour and mix all dry ingredients together, including any dry flavourings such as spices.

3 In a separate bowl, whisk together the milk, egg, oil and any wet ingredients such as frozen blueberries or mashed banana. Add to the dry ingredients and mix.

4 Bake for around 20 minutes (depending on the size of the muffin holes), until a skewer inserted comes out clean. Turn out onto a wire rack to cool.

5 Serve warm or cold.

suggested flavourings

Chopped dried apricots, nuts, seeds, lemon or orange zest, preserved ginger, chopped tinned fruit, frozen fruit, mashed banana, grated cheese, finely chopped onion, chopped cooked bacon, vanilla extract, ground nutmeg, ground cinnamon, dried herbs.

scones

Makes: 12 **Preparation:** 10 minutes **Cooking:** 10 minutes

250 g self-raising flour
1 teaspoon baking powder
pinch of salt
50 g butter, chopped into little pieces
150 ml milk
butter, or jam and cream, to serve

1 Preheat oven to 220°C and grease a baking tray.

2 Sift flour, baking powder and salt into a bowl. Add butter and rub in with your fingertips until the mixture resembles breadcrumbs. Add the milk and knead to a soft dough.

3 Place dough onto a floured board and, handling it as little as possible, gently pat out into a flat piece 3-cm thick.

4 Cut into squares, or make rounds using an inverted glass. Place on the baking tray. Brush with a little milk and bake for 10–12 minutes. Cool on a wire rack.

5 Serve warm or cold with butter, or jam and cream.

variation
For savoury scones, add 2 tablespoons grated cheese, finely chopped onion and/or cooked bacon, or ½ teaspoon dried herbs (oregano, thyme or marjoram).

For sweet scones, add 1 teaspoon sugar, plus 2 tablespoons chopped dates, currants or sultanas.

menu ideas

Cooking quick, afterwork meals using ingredients from your pantry doesn't have to be boring. In fact, cooking from a well-stocked pantry can be the impetus for a healthier and more varied diet. For example, instead of reaching for the cereal each morning, consider having baked beans or mashed sardines on wholemeal toast, or a bowl of oatmeal with stewed dried apricots with natural yoghurt.

The menu suggestions here show how varied your daily meals can be, using ingredients you have in your pantry. Simply pick up some salad ingredients or fresh vegetables on the weekend, make sure you have, plenty of staples, and your week's menu is sorted. Several special occasion menus are also included, for an impromptu dinner party or drinks with friends.

weekly menu

monday
Breakfast: Muffins – raspberry or apricot
Lunch: Onion Soup with savoury Damper
Dinner: Risotto with Bacon and Peas
Dessert: Golden Bread and Butter Pudding
Snacks: Poptastic Popcorn

tuesday
Breakfast: Savoury Omelette with Bacon
Lunch: Risotto Balls (made from last night's leftover risotto)
Dinner: Oliver's Olive Pasta, served with crusty bread and salad
Dessert: Apricot and Almond Pudding
Snacks: Savoury Palmiers

wednesday
Breakfast: Blueberry Pancakes
Lunch: Bean Salad in Pita Bread
Dinner: Poached Salmon in Thai Coconut Broth, with Fried Rice
Dessert: Cinnamon Crumble
Snacks: Scones, with jam and cream

thursday
Breakfast: Stewed dried apricots with natural yoghurt and oatmeal
(see Cheat's Trifle for how to stew dried apricots)
Lunch: Salmon Sandwiches
Dinner: Chickpea and Chorizo Casserole, with Polenta Wedges
Snack: Cheese Twists

friday

Breakfast: Cereal with extra chopped nuts, dried fruit and maple syrup

Lunch: Corn Chowder, with crusty bread

Dinner: Pizza with your choice of topping

Dessert: Frozen Berry Bombe

Snack: Anzac Biscuits

saturday

Breakfast: Corn Fritters, with tomato relish and bacon

Lunch: Tuna and Borlotti Bean Salad

Dinner: Fried Chicken Crispy Noodles

Dessert: Coconut Lemon Risotto

Snacks: Damper with dried fruit

sunday

Breakfast: Oatmeal porridge with berries

Lunch: Pissaladière

Dinner: Fish Cakes, with Lemon and Spinach Pilaf

Snack: All-purpose Butter Cake

special occasion menus

a drinks party
Cheese Twists
Ciabatta Crispbread
Hommus
Lentil Terrine
Savoury Palmiers
Sesame Chickpea Cannonballs
Spiced Nuts
White Bean Dip

a taste of asia
Sesame Prawn Toasts
Asian Chicken Dumpling Soup
Fried Chicken Crispy Noodles
Poached Salmon in Thai Coconut Broth
Garlic Prawns with Noodles
Fried Rice
Frozen Berry Bombe

an indian feast
Spiced Nuts (use spices such as ground
cumin, coriander and cardamom)
Pappadums
Vegetable Curry in a Flash
Indian Spiced Potato Patties
Lemon and Spinach Pilaf
Garlic Chickpeas
Apricot and Almond Pudding

shopping list

Photocopy this handy list and pin it to the inside of your pantry door.
Use as a source of inspiration, and as a checklist of stock items. Refer to it
before you go to the supermarket and you'll never have a bare pantry again!

shopping list

- [ ] allspice
- [ ] almonds - whole, ground, slivered
- [ ] anchovy fillets in oil *(tinned)*
- [ ] anchovy paste *(in a jar)*
- [ ] artichoke hearts in oil *(tinned or in a jar)*
- [ ] baby corn *(tinned)*
- [ ] bacon or pancetta *(frozen)*
- [ ] basil *(fresh and ground)*
- [ ] basil pesto *(in a jar)*
- [ ] bay leaves *(dried)*
- [ ] bean sprouts *(tinned)*
- [ ] beans – borlotti, butter, cannellini, pinto, red kidney, etc. *(dried or tinned)*
- [ ] beef stock *(cubes, frozen home-made, long-life liquid, or powdered)*
- [ ] beer

- [ ] beetroot *(tinned)*
- [ ] berries – blueberries, raspberries, strawberries, mixed, etc. *(frozen)*
- [ ] bicarbonate of soda
- [ ] black olive paste
- [ ] brandy (or other liqueur)
- [ ] bread *(fresh and frozen)*
- [ ] breadcrumbs
- [ ] broad beans *(frozen)*
- [ ] broccoli florets *(frozen)*
- [ ] burghul (cracked wheat)
- [ ] butter
- [ ] capers
- [ ] carrots *(fresh)*
- [ ] cashews
- [ ] castor sugar
- [ ] cayenne pepper
- [ ] cereal

- [ ] champignons *(tinned)*
- [ ] chanterelle mushrooms *(dried)*
- [ ] cheese – cheddar, mozzarella, parmesan, tasty, etc.
- [ ] chickpeas *(dried or tinned)*
- [ ] chicken fillets *(frozen)*
- [ ] chicken salt
- [ ] chicken stock *(cubes, frozen home-made, long-life liquid, or powdered)*
- [ ] chickpeas *(dried or tinned)*
- [ ] chilli *(dried flakes or ground)*
- [ ] Chinese crispy noodles
- [ ] chives *(dried and fresh)*
- [ ] chocolate *(block and chips)*
- [ ] chorizo (or similar cured spicy sausage)

shopping list

- [ ] cinnamon (*ground and sticks*)
- [ ] cloves
- [ ] coconut cream
- [ ] coconut milk
- [ ] coffee (*whole roasted beans and instant granules*)
- [ ] coriander (*fresh and ground*)
- [ ] corn chips
- [ ] corn kernels (*tinned or frozen*)
- [ ] cornflour
- [ ] couscous
- [ ] crab meat (*tinned*)
- [ ] crackers
- [ ] cream (*long-life*)
- [ ] cumin
- [ ] currants
- [ ] curry powder
- [ ] custard (*long-life or powdered*)

- [ ] dates
- [ ] Dijon mustard
- [ ] dried fruit – apricots, apples, etc.
- [ ] eggs
- [ ] egg or wheat noodles
- [ ] English mustard
- [ ] feta (*fresh*)
- [ ] fish fillets (*frozen*)
- [ ] fish sauce
- [ ] fish stock (*cubes, frozen home-made, long-life liquid, or powdered*)
- [ ] five-spice powder
- [ ] fruit – apricot, peaches, pears, cherries, etc. (*fresh and tinned*)
- [ ] garlic (*crushed in a jar, dried flakes, or fresh*)
- [ ] gherkins (*in a jar*)
- [ ] ginger (*crushed in a jar, fresh, or ground*)

- [ ] glass noodles or vermicelli (*dried*)
- [ ] golden syrup
- [ ] green beans (*frozen*)
- [ ] ham (*frozen*)
- [ ] harissa or chilli paste
- [ ] honey
- [ ] ice-cream
- [ ] icing sugar
- [ ] jalapeno peppers (*in a jar*)
- [ ] jams
- [ ] kaffir lime leaves (*dried*)
- [ ] lemon pepper
- [ ] lemons (*fresh and preserved*)
- [ ] lentils – red, green, yellow and/or brown (*dried or tinned*)
- [ ] lime pickle
- [ ] limes (*fresh*)
- [ ] mango chutney

shopping list

- [ ] maple syrup
- [ ] marjoram *(dried and fresh)*
- [ ] marmalade
- [ ] mayonnaise
- [ ] milk *(fresh and long-life)*
- [ ] mint *(dried and fresh)*
- [ ] mint jelly or sauce
- [ ] mixed herbs *(dried)*
- [ ] mushrooms *(dried or tinned)*
- [ ] nutmeg
- [ ] olive oil – virgin and extra virgin, and/or flavoured
- [ ] olives – green and black, pitted, stuffed and whole
- [ ] onions – brown and red *(dried flakes and fresh)*
- [ ] onion marmalade

- [ ] oregano *(dried and fresh)*
- [ ] panettoni
- [ ] paprika
- [ ] parsley *(dried and fresh)*
- [ ] passata
- [ ] pasta – butterfly, macaroni, penne, dried spirals, spinach, etc.
- [ ] peanut butter
- [ ] peanut oil
- [ ] peanuts (unsalted)
- [ ] peas *(dried or frozen)*
- [ ] peppercorns – black
- [ ] pine nuts
- [ ] pita bread
- [ ] plain flour – white and wholemeal
- [ ] polenta
- [ ] popcorn kernels
- [ ] poppy seeds

- [ ] porcini mushrooms *(dried)*
- [ ] potatoes *(fresh)*
- [ ] prawns *(frozen or tinned)*
- [ ] puff pastry *(frozen)*
- [ ] pumpkin *(fresh)*
- [ ] raisins
- [ ] red capsicum slices in oil
- [ ] rice – Arborio, basmati, brown, jasmine, long and short grain, etc.
- [ ] rice wine or mirin
- [ ] rolled oats
- [ ] rosemary *(dried and fresh)*
- [ ] saffron *(powder or threads)*
- [ ] salad greens
- [ ] salami
- [ ] salmon *(tinned)*

shopping list

- [ ] sardines in oil or brine *(tinned)*
- [ ] satay sauce
- [ ] sea salt
- [ ] self-raising flour – white and wholemeal
- [ ] semolina
- [ ] sesame oil
- [ ] sesame seeds
- [ ] sherry
- [ ] shortcrust pastry *(frozen)*
- [ ] sour cream
- [ ] souvlaki bread
- [ ] soy sauce
- [ ] spaghetti and fettuccine
- [ ] spinach *(frozen)*
- [ ] sponge fingers
- [ ] star anise
- [ ] sugar – soft brown, castor, icing and raw

- [ ] sultanas
- [ ] sun-dried tomatoes
- [ ] sweet chilli sauce
- [ ] sweet potatoes *(fresh)*
- [ ] tahini
- [ ] tapenade
- [ ] tea – black, green, herbal, etc. *(bags and leaf)*
- [ ] Thai curry paste – green and red
- [ ] thyme *(dried and fresh)*
- [ ] tomatoes – chopped, crushed, diced, whole peeled, etc. *(tinned)*
- [ ] tomato paste *(sachets or in a jar)*
- [ ] tomato relish
- [ ] tomato sauce
- [ ] tuna – in oil or brine *(tinned)*
- [ ] turmeric

- [ ] vanilla *(extract, essence or beans)*
- [ ] vegetable oil (or canola or sunflower oil)
- [ ] vegetable stock *(cubes, frozen home-made, long-life liquid, or powdered)*
- [ ] Vegemite
- [ ] vinegar – balsamic, cider, redand/or white wine
- [ ] walnuts
- [ ] water chestnuts *(tinned)*
- [ ] wholegrain mustard
- [ ] wine – white and red
- [ ] Worcestershire sauce
- [ ] yeast
- [ ] yoghurt (natural)

index